ROBERT SCHUMANN

Robert Schumann

ROBERT SCHUMANN
1810-1856

BY

J. A. FULLER–MAITLAND

FOREWORD BY
FRANCESCO BERGER
HON, R.A.M., F.G.S.M.

KENNIKAT PRESS
Port Washington, N. Y./London

ROBERT SCHUMANN

First published in 1913
Reissued in 1970 by Kennikat Press
Library of Congress Catalog Card No: 73-102841
SBN 8046-0760-5

Manufactured by Taylor Publishing Company   Dallas, Texas

SCHUMANN

SCHUMANN was a poet, a dreamer, a thoroughly unpractical man, and, at times, an impossible one.

His life was uneventful. There is little adventure or incident in it, and consequently not much for the biographer to tell. He had no *petits amours*, travelled but little, and then not far.

The two outstanding features in his career are his romantic attachment to his wife Clara, warmly reciprocated by her, and the gradual but fatal decay of his mentality. Had he been granted more years for further development of his inborn genius, he would have bequeathed to us a larger number of Works showing more complete mastery of workmanship than he was permitted to do. For the genius that conceives is not always the genius that knows how to present its creations in the most acceptable form, and to this combination of two separate qualities, Schumann did not at all times attain. Hence a considerable portion of his larger Works, and of his longer pianoforte pieces, sound more tentative and experimental than perfected models should sound. It is in his smaller or shorter ones, his songs and certain pianoforte pieces only, that we find so much to admire and so little to condone.

The blemishes here referred to, which further experience would probably have rectified, may perhaps be accounted for by the fact that, as fast as he wrote for the pianoforte, his gifted wife was at hand with her interpretative skill, to enhance their attractiveness, and to omit what was not attractive.

He was splendidly critical of others, witness his generous appreciation of Mendelssohn, Bennett, Chopin and Brahms, but seems to have been singularly devoid of self-criticism; in this respect, as indeed in many others, differing widely from his contemporaries just named. Nor was his contempt of minor pianist-composers always justifiable, nor his depreciation of Italian opera composers always reasonable.

Few men's lives have been so closely interwoven with the influence of their wives as his. Not as the devoted consort only, nor as the model mother of his children, but additionally as his brilliant and indefatigable propagandist, is Clara Schumann inseparably identified with his career. The recognition of his genius and acceptance of his music at an earlier date than might otherwise have happened, are largely due to her efforts.

In illustration of how a true artist's work is endless, it may be here mentioned that during one of her latest visits to England in her seventieth year, a mutual friend, at whose house she was staying, remarked to the writer that he was being driven nearly mad by her *incessant practice* of certain passages in her husband's Concerto, which she was announced to play at a forthcoming concert. After fifty years of repeated success, she was still labouring to perfect herself to her own satisfaction!

Though opinions vary about some of Schumann's works, there is complete agreement as to the merits of others. His superb pianoforte Concerto, his Toccata, Novelletten, and Etudes Symphoniques are brilliant examples of genius, destined to immortalise his name, and make us lament how limited is his number of Works of equal quality.

F. B.

CONTENTS.

CHAPTER VIII.

ROBERT SCHUMANN

CHAPTER I.

THE TWENTY YEARS' WAR.

1810—1830.

"My whole life has been a twenty years' war between prose and poetry—between law and music."
Schumann's letter to his mother, 1830.

INTERESTING as it is, in beginning a musical biography, to trace the artistic faculty back through generations of highly-gifted ancestors, and to establish the position that genius, like insanity, is hereditary, there are many cases where it is impossible to do this. In some instances, as notably in that of the Bach family, musical ability was a second nature to every scion of the house, so that to be a Bach was to be a musician. Theirs was an exceptional, not to say unique, case in the history of music. It is not uncommon to find, that among the progenitors of a composer there have been individuals who had a liking for music, or even a more decided taste for it. In the Schumann family however, no musical ancestor has been discovered by any of his biographers, and we may take it for granted that no such existed.

The composer's father, Friedrich August Gottlob Schumann (born 1773), was the son of a clergyman in Saxony, Friedrich Gottlob Schumann by name, who designed for his son a commercial career. After a long and wearisome period of tutelage, August Schumann determined to abandon the idea of a mercantile life, and to adopt a profession more congenial to his literary tastes; these were by no means small, and they had been fostered during a short period of study at the university of Leipzig, where a situation in a commercial establishment had been obtained by him. One Heinse, a bookseller, offered him a subordinate place in his employ, and Schumann accepted the situation, as affording him the opportunity of learning the trade that he wished to adopt, and also of improving his knowledge and culture in the atmosphere of books. Here he became acquainted with the daughter of the chief surgeon of Zeitz, Johanna Christiana Schnabel, who afterwards became his wife. Before the marriage could take place, it was necessary for Schumann to found a firm of his own; in order therefore to procure the requisite capital, he returned to business, went into partnership in the year 1795 with a merchant of Nonneburg, and soon afterwards was in a position to marry and set up as a bookseller. He now took one of his brothers into partnership, and established the firm of " Schumann Brothers," which lasted from 1808 till 1840, in the Saxon town of Zwickau.

Neither he nor his wife seems to have had any remarkable love of, or aptitude for, the art to which they were the means of giving so distinguished an ornament. All that is on record concerning August Schumann's literary attainments is that he had a decided love of the *belles lettres,* being especially fond of the poems of Milton and Young, and that he published translations of Byron's " Childe Harold " and " Beppo." He also wrote some treatises on commercial and other subjects, which obtained a certain degree of celebrity.

The mother seems to have been a person of an eminently practical disposition; though entirely lacking in imagination, she was much addicted to that kind of romantic sentimentality which is only found to perfection in minds of a thoroughly common-place type.

Four children, Edward, Karl, Julius, and Emilie, were born to the Schumanns before the birth of Robert Alexander, which took place on June 8, 1810, in the house at Zwickau, No. 5, on the market-place. The youngest survived the rest, the sister dying in her twentieth year in a condition of nervous melancholy which bordered closely on insanity.

From his father Robert Schumann seems to have inherited, together with a certain delicacy of constitution, his keenness of perception, imaginative nature, and sensitive disposition; while his mother's predilections may be held responsible for her son's romantic tendencies.

His general education began in his sixth year at the school of Archdeacon Döhner in his native town ; his first lessons in music were received in the following year from one of the professors at the High School of

Zwickau, J. G. Kuntsch. As this teacher had risen from a very low condition and was entirely self-taught, we may conclude that his method was not all that might have been desired ; his pupil, however, conceived an affection for him which lasted for many years, for in 1852 we find him writing to his old master of thirty-five years before in terms of the highest esteem and most grateful affection.   It was at this time that he began to amuse himself and his companions by giving musical expression to their various peculiarities on the piano.   The extraordinary skill with which he perceived their characteristics, to say nothing of the musical ability that such a feat presupposes, shows that even at this childish age his insight into human nature must have been extraordinarily developed.

In the summer of 1819, his father took him to Carlsbad, where he heard Moscheles play, an event of which he preserved the liveliest recollection in after-life.   When the boy was ten years old, he was entered in the fourth class of the Zwickau Academy, where he remained until 1828.   Here he formed the first of his many musical friendships with the son of a musician named Piltzing, in whose society he explored the great world of compositions of all schools, so far as they were procurable by the boys, in the form of pianoforte arrangements.   In this, as in many similar undertakings, the elder Schumann gave his son every encouragement that lay in his power, laying in a stock of standard compositions for the boy's benefit.   The discovery, among these last, of the orchestral parts of Righini's overture to " Tigranes," incited the friends to form a small band for the performance of this work;

and such of their schoolfellows as had a love of music
were at once enlisted in the project, the result being
that a performance took place under Robert's direction,
who not only conducted, but filled in all the missing
parts on the piano. The entire strength of this first
orchestra of Schumann's consisted of seven players—
two violins, two flutes, a clarionet, and two horns.
This inaugural meeting was followed by many similar
ones, at some, if not all of which, compositions by
Schumann himself were played to a small but appreciative audience, consisting solely of the boy's father.
His appearances were not entirely limited, however, to
this very exclusive circle : when he was about eleven
years old he accompanied, standing up at the piano to
do so, at a public performance of Schneider's " Welt-
gericht," which was conducted by Kuntsch. His fame
as a pianist and extempore player became known in
his native town, and his father, who, from having been
thwarted in his own choice of a profession in early life,
was well able to sympathize with his son's artistic
desires, resolved, notwithstanding his wife's remon-
strances, to make a musician of him. With this object
in view, he wrote to C. M. von Weber, at that time
Capellmeister in Dresden, asking him to undertake
his son's musical education. This Weber agreed to do,
but the project came to nothing ; and the death of
August Schumann in 1825 put a stop to the idea of
Robert's adopting the artistic life ; for the prejudices
of the mother were now unopposed.

At this time the inordinately high spirits which
characterized his childhood forsook him gradually,
giving way to a melancholy disposition, from which

henceforth he never was entirely free. Doubtless the
change in his temperament was due in no small degree
to the absence of his father's encouragement in his
artistic development. What he lacked at home was in
some measure made up for by the kindness and geniality
of a family with whom he became very intimate at this
time, that of Dr. Carus, who was afterwards professor
of medicine in the universities of Leipzig and Dorpat,
and whose wife, an enthusiastic lover of music, found
a congenial friend in Schumann. With this lady he
enjoyed, to use his own expression, "perfect revels of
song;" he also made sundry experiments in song-
writing on his own account.

At this time he made his first acquaintance with the
writings of Jean Paul, and passed through a phase of
transcendentalism, writing a good deal of poetry and
setting it to music of his own. In March, 1828, the
mother, having found a partisan in Robert's guardian,
a certain merchant named Rudel, determined to force
her son into the legal profession, and with that in-
tent sent him off to Leipzig, where he matriculated as
studiosus juris. Through two former friends—Flechsig
and Semmel by name—he now became acquainted
with a fellow-student named Gisbert Rosen, with whom
he rapidly became very intimate, for he found that
Rosen thoroughly sympathized with him in his devoted
admiration of Jean Paul. In April, only a month
after his matriculation, when Rosen was quitting
Leipzig for Heidelberg, Schumann bore him company,
and invited him to stay at his own home, and after a
short visit the friends resumed their journey, Schumann
going only as far as Munich. The stay here was

marked by a great event in the youth's life, an introduction to Heine, who received the friends very kindly,
delighting them with his brilliant conversation. At
Augsburg, on his way to Munich, Schumann had a first
experience of the tender passion. His host in that
town, Dr. Kurrer, to whom the travellers had brought
a letter of introduction, had a pretty daughter called
Clara, and with this young lady Schumann fell at
once in love, in spite of the fact that she was already
engaged to be married. His passion seems to have
been of the most platonic and transcendental kind, for
the betrothed lover was cognizant of the affair throughout, and made no sort of objection. After the friends
had parted at Munich, and Schumann had gone back to
his books at Leipzig, he made frequent allusions to
the lovely Clara in his correspondence with Rosen, but
the flame soon burnt itself out.

At Leipzig, Schumann found that he could not altogether relinquish music and poetry for his studies : he
wrote to Rosen that he has "not been to a single
lecture, but has worked by himself ;" this he explains
to mean that he has "played the piano and written
some Jean-Pauliads." His friends, the Caruses, having
by this time come to Leipzig, Schumann resumed his
old intimacy with them, and at their house had the
advantage of meeting many interesting people, chief
among whom were Marschner the composer, and, most
important for his future life, Friedrich Wieck, whose
pupil he soon afterwards became. No doubt he was
attracted to him, in part at least, by the extraordinary
playing of his elder daughter, named, like the romantic
youth's first love, Clara. By this time, though she was

only nine years old, she had made such wonderful progress under her father, as to warrant her appearing in public ; and two years afterwards, we hear of her making a musical tour. Since the gifted lady is, happily, still before the public to bear witness to the excellence of her father's early training, we need not doubt that Schumann profited to a very great degree by his instructions, even though they were not of long duration. For at Easter 1829, Schumann went to Heidelberg, ostensibly to complete his legal studies, but inwardly resolved to become a musician, should any opportunity present itself. Under Wieck he had devoted his energies entirely to the technique of the art, neglecting his master's urgent advice that he should improve his scanty theoretical knowledge ; and yet, in spite of his contempt for the science of music, his favourite composers were not only Schubert, who had just died, and in whose works Schumann and his friends took a keen interest, but Bach, whose compositions, one would think, would fire any one with the necessary energy to undertake the scientific part of musical study. During this phase he wrote some four-hand Polonaises, a Quartet for piano and strings, and some songs, all unpublished. In a little more than a year from this time, after his technical acquirements had been rendered useless by the accident which turned the whole course of his artistic career, he bitterly regretted having worked so exclusively at the mechanical branch of the art, and wished that he had the time over again to give to the theoretical studies which he had neglected.

No doubt the move to Heidelberg was undertaken

in deference to his mother's wishes, for she was probably dissatisfied with the young student's progress in the law, and perhaps thought he would be less exposed to temptations of a musical kind in a new sphere. The chief purpose of his going cannot, as some have thought, have been to renew his intimacy with Rosen, for the latter's time was finished, and it was only by a piece of good fortune that he managed to stay on in the university, and thus to resume his interrupted intercourse with Schumann. In the transit between the two universities, Schumann spent the Easter holidays on visits to his relations at Zwickau and Schneeberg, and in a letter written to Rosen from the latter place we see that the many festivities given by his friends in his honour succeeded in effacing to a great extent the regrets which he felt at leaving Leipzig. On May 2nd he started for Heidelberg, but he was induced to make a détour, by the accidental companionship of the poet Willibald Alexis, with whom the impulsive youth was so charmed, that he went for some distance down the Rhine in his company, and thus did not reach Heidelberg or his friend till the end of the month. The learned Thibaut undertook the superintendence of Schumann's studies, but poor Pegasus would not work in harness; Schumann felt an ever-increasing distaste for the learned profession for which he was intended. Though Thibaut's lectures failed to inspire in him any reverence for the study of jurisprudence, he was attracted by another side of his teacher's knowledge, for in after-years we find him recommending to all young musicians the frequent study of his quondam preceptor's admirable

contribution to musical literature, the treatise "On
Purity in Musical Art"—"Ueber Reinheit der Ton-
kunst." In a little time Thibaut had the wisdom to
perceive his pupil's true vocation, and to advise him
to embrace the musical profession. Not that it re-
quired any wonderful degree of perspicacity to see
that Schumann could never make a good lawyer, for
he himself always expressed his dislike of the subject
with the utmost freedom. It must not be imagined
that he passed his time at Heidelberg in idleness; he
continued his study of the pianoforte technique with
the greatest diligence, and during the excursions that
he made in the neighbourhood with his friends Rosen
and Semmel, the latter of whom had come to the
university, much to Schumann's gratification, he took
a dumb keyboard in the carriage and practised five-
finger exercises constantly. It would seem that this
contrivance did him very little good, for in the advice
to young musicians, from which we have already
quoted, he advises the student to try such inventions
"just to see how useless they are." The friends longed
to extend their travels, and to make a tour in North
Italy. When the summer vacation began, Schumann
wrote to his guardian, Rudel, to ask for the necessary
supplies, and for permission to go. Some difficulty
was at first made at home, for the young man had not
been particularly economical during his university life;
but ultimately permission was given, and he started;
his friends, however, failed him at the last moment,
and he had to go alone. The journey, which extended
as far as Venice, was by no means devoid of incident,
to judge from several letters to Rosen and to Therese,

the wife of his eldest brother Eduard; in these, which are given in Wasielewski's life, we hear of a very transient passion for a charming English girl whom he met in Milan, and who presented him, at parting, with a branch of cypress; of a dispute in a Venetian restaurant with a gentleman of Hebrew extraction, which, happily, was without serious consequences of any kind; of a short attack of illness; and, more than all else, of his first hearing Paganini.

On his return to Heidelberg, after some difficulties with importunate creditors, he continued his piano studies with renewed ardour; a new friend, a student named Töpken, being admitted to the circle of his intimates. During this winter, too, he went into society more than he had hitherto done, and was received with open arms in the musical world of the place. One public appearance, at which he played the " Alexander Variations " of Moscheles, took place at Heidelberg, but most of the invitations received by him for public performances were refused.

Among the musical productions which date from this time, are some of the pieces afterwards collected into the work called " Papillons," the variations on the name *Abegg*, and a good many sketches, one among them being for the Toccata (op. 7), which was then projected in D major. About this time Schumann went to Frankfort, and heard Paganini again to his great delight. The impression produced on him by the great violinist resulted in the arrangement for the pianoforte of his studies and caprices; and an agreeable episode, in the shape of a meeting with a young lady named Meta Abegg, which took place at a ball at Mannheim, was preserved in the variations on her surname, as represented by the notes A, B flat, E, G, G. On his return, since his chance of distinguishing himself in the approaching law examination was very small indeed, he resolved to induce his mother to withdraw her objections, and to allow him to devote himself to music. After some discussion with her and his guardian, in which the mother took the view that her son had not sufficient talent to ensure his artistic success, the question was referred to Wieck. He gave the answer that Schumann so eagerly hoped to hear, and it was resolved, to his unspeakable joy, that he should become a pianist by profession. He looked forward to six years of hard work before he would be fit to appear in public; but this was as nothing compared with the tedious suspense of his life up to this point, which, as he tells his mother in a letter on the all-important subject, "had been a twenty years' war between prose and poetry—betwen law and music."

The war was now at an end; henceforward Schumann lived for art alone.

CHAPTER II.

THE ARTIST'S DEVELOPMENT.

1830—1843.

" Out of weakness made strong."

IN the summer and autumn of 1830 Schumann's prospects, which in the event proved so illusory, were at their brightest. With the dearest wish of his heart realized, released from the obnoxious studies, and free to follow that vocation for which he imagined that he was best fitted, he saw himself on the threshold of a glorious career, and felt that when he had once overcome those technical difficulties connected with the pianoforte, which were as yet insuperable by him, he would be ready to launch himself into the great world of music. He determined to put himself in the hands of his old teacher, Wieck, and with that object went back to Leipzig, where he was fortunate enough to obtain rooms in Wieck's own house, Grimmaische Gasse, No. 36. Here he remained until the autumn of 1832. He soon, however, became discontented with his rate of progress, and fondly imagined that he could arrive at the desired perfection by a royal road of his own invention. He gave up his lessons with Wieck and pursued his plan in entire secrecy. Though the exact details of the invention were never revealed, it is known what were its object and mode of operation. In order to gain equality of strength and independence in all the fingers, he fastened the third finger, the weakest of all, in a strained position, and then practised diligently with the others. When the time came for the release of the finger and the demonstration of the success of the operation, he found to his horror that the third finger was useless, and indeed that his whole right hand, to which alone the invention had been applied, was practically crippled. Every remedy was tried, but in vain. For a long time he did not give up hoping for a cure, and meanwhile he practised assiduously with the left hand, in expectation of the time when his right should be restored to him. This recovery never took place, and it was well for music that it was so, for in losing a pianist whose powers, however great, could only have delighted his contemporaries, the art gained a composer, whose conceptions will rejoice the hearts of all generations till the end of time.

Though all his hopes of success as a virtuoso were thus dashed to the ground, Schumann did not lose courage, but, believing in his own powers as a composer, determined to begin over again in a new branch of art, and to pursue those theoretical studies that he had once despised and disliked. His teacher in composition was not Wieck, but Heinrich Dorn, who was at that time conductor of the Leipzig opera. Under him Schumann had to begin with the most elementary studies, his first task being to harmonize a chorale in four parts. He made rapid progress, and benefited to the full by Dorn's instructions. The first-fruits of his labour in the new profession were the "Papillons," which he had begun in the previous year, and which he now completed, dedicating them to his three sisters-in-law, Therese, Rosalie, and Emilie, the last of whom must not be confused with his own sister of the same name, who had died before this. It was not until the next year, 1831, that his right hand became so hopelessly lame as to make it a matter of absolute certainty that he would never be able to play, or at least to become a public performer. What he felt concerning this downfall of all his early hopes, just when the difficulties that formerly stood in his way were overcome, we know from a letter written by him to his friend Töpken, on Good Friday, 1833, in which he refers to the folly of striving after a perfection of technique, which can only be acquired by long patience, and not by artificial expedients. He says, " we grasp the handle so tightly that the vessel is shattered." But still he makes light of the accident itself, and he naively lets us into the secret of his comparative indifference to the condition of his hand by alluding to " a great orchestral symphony ;" and from other passages in the letter, which is given entire in the original German of Wasielewski's life, we see that the new artistic aspirations and ideals had by this time begun to make up for the loss he had sustained.

In this year Schumann made his first attempt at musical criticism. He had become acquainted with Chopin's variations on " La ci darem la mano," which had just been published in Vienna as the composer's Opus 2, and he thereupon wrote a somewhat fancifu eulogy on the work, and sent it to the *Allgemeine Musikalische Zeitung,* in which periodical it appeared, much to the astonishment, no doubt, of the regular readers of the paper; for a wilder, more rhapsodical piece of writing, calling itself a musical criticism, never was in this world before. The imaginary characters of Florestan and Eusebius, who make their first appearance in this article, and of whom more anon, cannot have given much assistance to an uninitiated public, desiring to understand and enter into the sentiments of the writer concerning Chopin. The article, which appears in vol. xxxiii., No 49 of the paper, is re-published, and forms the first of the collected writings of Schumann.

In the winter of 1832-33 he paid visits to his relations at Zwickau and Schneeberg, staying in the former town for some time, and working hard at composition. Besides the " Intermezzos " and the Paganini Caprices, both of which date from this time, we hear of a symphony in G minor, the first movement of which was played both at Zwickau and Schneeberg during the winter; the whole work was given in 1835 at Zwickau, but it has never since been heard of by the world, nor was it ever published. The first performance of the opening movement of the work in his native town took place on an occasion most memorable to Schumann, for it was at a concert given by Clara Wieck, who was then thirteen years old. Schumann, as we may well believe, was enraptured by her exquisite playing, though of course he can scarcely have regarded her with feelings of a warmer kind, considering her tender age. In March, 1833, he returned to Leipzig, though not to Wieck's house: he took up his residence in a house in Riedel's garden. While here he seems to have worked hard in the daytime, though not with any teacher, and to have received his intimates in the evenings, or joined their festive gatherings at the "Kaffeebaum" restaurant; not that he was a very sociable member of the company, for he generally sat quite silently, taking or seeming to take little interest in what was going forward. While he was in these picturesque surroundings he completed the set of studies after Paganini's Caprices, the Toccata, re-modelled and transposed from D to C major, and wrote a set of Impromptus on an air by Clara Wieck, which were afterwards published as op. 5. In the autumn, probably because the weather made the garden-house less to be desired than in the summer, he changed his place of abode, and took lodgings in No. 21, Burg-strasse, on the fourth story. Here the news of his sister-in-law Rosalie's death on October 17 reached him and produced a severe attack of nervous mental excite-ment, during which he seems to have suffered exceed-ingly. It may be surmised that it was a foreshadowing of the doom which was ultimately to obscure his mind, for according to one account he made an attempt to throw himself out of the window. However this may be, it is certain that in after-life he had the greatest objection to sleeping in a room on an upper floor.

At the end of this year several new friendships were formed, chief amongst which were those with a painter named Lyser and with Ludwig Schunke, a musician of considerable talent, with whom Schumann speedily became intimate.

These friends, together with some others, assisted
Schumann in projecting the musical periodical which
engrossed so much of his attention about this time.
In the preface to his collected works, he describes how
the young musical enthusiasts among whom he was
thrown agreed in deploring the existing state of music
in Germany. We hear how "the stage was ruled by
Rossini, and the pianoforte by Herz and Hünten, almost
to the exclusion of every one else. And yet only a
few years had passed since Beethoven, Weber, and
Schubert lived amongst us." One day the young enthusiasts were struck with a bright idea: "Let us no
longer look on idly, let us try to make things better,
so that the poetry of art may once more be duly
honoured." Thus arose the first pages of the *Neue
Zeitschrift für Musik*. We must remember that at
this time the only musical criticism in Germany was
of the most futile kind. Silly, superficial admiration
of mediocrity—Schumann used to call it "honey-
daubing" ("Honigpinselei")—or contemptuous depreciation of what was new or unknown, these were the
order of the day in such of the journals as deigned to
notice music at all, and even in the *Allgemeine Musi
kalische Zeitung* the state of things was not much
better.

When the new literary venture was launched upon
the world—the first number appeared on April 3rd,
1834—Schumann was assisted in bringing it out by
Schunke before-mentioned, Friedrich Wieck, and a
clever man of letters, a certain Julius Knorr. It was
not until the summer of this year that they secured
the valuable help of Carl Banck, who came from Berlin

at this time, partly in order to take part in the new
scheme, and whose influence brought many admirable
contributors into the undertaking.

We must now introduce the reader to two female
friends of Schumann's, who exercised considerable influence over him at this and subsequent periods. His
friend Schunke had introduced him to Frau Henriette
Voigt, the wife of a merchant in Leipzig, an accom-
plished, cultivated lady, and altogether a friend after
Schumann's own heart. He found in her a spirit akin
to his own, and remained on terms of the greatest
intimacy with her until her early death in 1839. The
other friendship was of a more romantic kind, and was
also of much shorter duration. A young lady named
Ernestine von Fricken had lately come to Leipzig, in
order to complete her study of the pianoforte under
Wieck, in whose house she, like Schumann before her,
took up her abode. If we may believe Wasielewski,
she had not any surpassing attractions, either physical
or intellectual, which would account for Schumann's
ardent affection for her, and we therefore need not
wonder that his love should have proved very transient,
especially when we remember that within a couple of
years from this time, he had conceived the real love of
his life, for her who was to him a faithful friend and a
devoted wife, as well as a keen sympathizer with all his
artistic ideals.

For the sake of all students of Schumann's musical
and critical writings, it will be convenient in this
place to give a complete list, so far as it is known, of
the various pseudonyms adopted by Schumann for himself and his friends, as well as those used by his friends

as *noms de plume* in their contributions to the paper.
Some of the names occur only in Schumann's writings,
others only in his compositions, but it is most convenient to give the entire list now.

"Florestan" . . . Schumann. The name represents the
turbulent and impulsive side of his
nature, full of imaginative activity.

"Eusebius" . . . Schumann. The character is an em-
bodiment of the gentle, thoughtful,
and sensitive qualities in the composer.

"Meister Raro" . . Schumann. This character stands between the two former, acting as
moderator in their frequent disputes,
and sometimes as judge, summing
up after their opposing criticisms
have been uttered. The name is
sometimes applied to F. Wieck.

"Jeanquirit" . . . Schumann. A name subscribed occasionally, but comparatively rarely,
to some criticisms written in a light
and humorous style.

"Serpentinus" . .
"B." . . . . . } Carl Banck
"C——k." . . .

"Julius" . . . } Julius Knorr.
"Knif" . . . .

"Jonathan" . . . Ludwig Schunke, sometimes Schumann.
"Fritz Friedrich" . Lyser the painter.
"Gottschalk Wedel" Anton von Zuccalmaglio.
"Felix Meritis" . . F. Mendelssohn-Bartholdy.
"Walt" . . . . (?) The name occurs only once; it is taken
from Jean Paul's "Flegeljahre."

"Chiarina" . . .
"Zilia" . . . . } Clara Wieck.
"Cecilia" . . . .

"Eleanore" . . . } Henriette Voigt.
"Aspasia" . . . .

"Estrelle" . . . . Ernestine von Fricken.
"Giulietta" . . . Livia Gerhardt, a clever singer, who
afterwards married Dr. Frege.

The leading spirits of the undertaking were accustomed to sign their contributions very often with

certain combinations of figures. The figure 1 indicates that Knorr is the author; 2, 12, 22, 32, are adopted by Schumann himself; 3 by Schunke; and 6, 16, 26 &c.,.by Carl Banck.

These, with some kindred souls, among whom were Berlioz and Chopin, were one and all, with or without their knowledge, incorporated in a certain mystical community of Schumann's own invention, familiar to students of his compositions under the name of the "Davidsbund." The bond of union in this society, which, as Schumann himself tells us, "existed only in the head of its founder," was the determination to do battle in the cause of musical progress against Philistinism in every form. The "Davidsbund" has been well compared to the "Pre-Raphaelite Brotherhood" in England, and this comparison is perhaps the best explanation that could be given of the aims and objects of Schumann and his friends.

Of Schumann's own work as an author we shall have occasion to speak more fully in a later chapter. So much as this it was necessary to say concerning the "Davidsbund" and the *Neue Zeitschrift,* in order to explain the constant references with which we shall meet in the letters dating from this time.

The year which saw the projection and commencement of the *Neue Zeitschrift* was, as we might expect, not particularly rich in musical productions. But though the works produced and sketched were small in quantity—the "Études Symphoniques" were completed and the "Carnaval" begun—as far as quality is concerned they were surpassed by none of the composer's pianoforte works. Both compositions will be examined in detail later. But we may remark in passing, that both contain evidences which prove that he was, or fancied himself, deeply in love with Mdlle. von Fricken at the time when the works were composed. The "Études" are written on a theme composed by the lady's father, and a very beautiful theme it is; and the "Carnaval" contains, besides a little piece supposed to represent her character, constant reference to a phrase of four notes, which in their German nomenclature spell the word *Asch*, the name of the little village in Bohemia from which the fair one had come to Leipzig. The second of these compositions was not finished till the following year, by which time he had sustained a loss which deeply affected him, his friend Schunke having died of consumption in the winter, while Schumann was on a visit to his relations at Zwickau. In a letter to Joseph Fischhof, given by Wasielewski, he informs him of Schunke's death in words which show how much it affected him, and at the same time he requests Fischhof to help him in the conduct of the paper. Accordingly we find Fischhof shortly after this acting as Schumann's colleague, although he lived at Vienna.

In October, 1835, the arrival of Mendelssohn in Leipzig gave a new interest to Schumann's life. The two great composers met for the first time on October 3rd, at the house of Friedrich Wieck, the day before Mendelssohn conducted his first concert at the Gewandhaus. Moscheles was also in Leipzig at the time, and was present at the frequent meetings of which that just mentioned was the first. During the next two or three years the two artists were on terms of the greatest cordiality. Schumann's feeling for Mendelssohn was one of genuine and unbounded admiration, a feeling which was by no means reciprocated, although Mendelssohn recognized in Schumann a kindred spirit so far as artistic ideals were concerned. The opinions of each concerning the other will be given when we come to examine Schumann's relations with his critics, and with those whom he criticized.

In was in the spring of the following year that he began to regard Clara Wieck in another light than that of a gifted artist, and to turn his wandering affections in that direction from which they never afterwards swerved. In consequence of a long separation from the object of his affection, while she was away on a concert tour with her father, Schumann had no opportunity of declaring his love, though he managed to establish a correspondence through a friend and fellow-worker on the paper, a certain August Kahlert, until the summer of 1837, when his proposal, made to Wieck, was received by no means favourably, although it was not absolutely rejected. The father held that the prospects of the young composer were not sufficiently certain to allow of his marrying. He may also have cherished hopes of a more ambitious kind for his daughter. In order to render his pecuniary circumstances more satisfactory, Schumann conceived the project of going to Vienna, and establishing his periodical in that city, there being no musical paper of any kind there. In a letter to Zuccalmaglio, dated August 8th, 1838, given in the appendix to Mr. Hueffer's " Music of the Future," he says, " I hope to derive much good from this change; a new round of

c

life, new work, and new ideas. I shall have many
troubles to get over; and we have to go on rather
gently, as the censorship is strict and will suppress
freely." Schumann of course thought that he was
going into a world of music, where that opposition to all
artistic progress which has always been a distinctive
characteristic of the musical society of Leipzig would
no longer be felt, and where he should meet with
enthusiastic support and sympathy in his literary and
artistic schemes. But these hopes were dashed to the
ground when he came to know the real state of music
in Vienna, the city which of all others deserves the
name of the city of music. Here, where Haydn, Mozart, Beethoven, and Schubert had lived and worked,
there was little trace of their influence. The attractive
trivialities of Strauss in the sphere of instrumental
music, and of Proch and his followers in vocal music,
were the only compositions that the people cared to
hear.

In spite of his disappointment with the Viennese
public, and the many difficulties caused by the censorship, he did not relinquish the idea of bringing out the
Neue Zeitschrift in Vienna until the spring of the
next year, 1839, when, seeing that the case was hope-
less, he came back to Leipzig. He brought two trea-
sures home with him; one was the score of Schubert's
Symphony in C major, which was entrusted to his care
by the composer's brother Ferdinand, and which
Schumann got performed at the Gewandhaus on March
21st. The other treasure was a steel pen, which
Schumann, who dearly loved anything that savoured
of sentimental mysticism, found lying upon the grave

of Beethoven in Währing cemetery, and which he kept, regarding it as a portent of unusual good, and using it on very special occasions, as for instance when writing the score of the Symphony in B flat, and the notice of Schubert's C major Symphony for the *Zeitschrift*.

On his return home he renewed and improved his friendship with Sterndale Bennett, who had come to Leipzig shortly before Schumann went away. But with this exception he made no new friends, for he was engrossed in his attempts to obtain the consent of Wieck to his union with Clara, attempts which were only crowned with success after a long and tedious lawsuit, which resulted in the necessary permission being absolutely forced out of the obdurate parent. The lovers, after having waited in a state of the most painful suspense, were at last happily married on September 12th, 1840, in the church of Schönefeld, near Leipzig. Shortly before his marriage the degree of Doctor of Philosophy was conferred upon him by the University of Jena. Eight children were the fruit of this marriage, all of whom survived Schumann.

The various difficulties and disappointments through which he had gone since he first declared his affection, had borne fruit in his musical creations. All the finest of his pianoforte works date from these years. It would seem that he had resolved to attain to the perfection of form as a writer for the piano before attempting any other branch of composition. True, there are a few essays in other directions, as, for instance, the Symphony in G minor; but of the works which we now possess, all the greatest of those written for the piano are earlier in date than any other class of his works.

The period which immediately succeeded the marriage was one of quiet, happy work. In the profound retirement which he enjoyed almost without interruption for the next four years, he studied every new form of composition, making himself master of each in turn, and leaving in each works which in truth deserve the epithet "monumental." In 1840, the year of his marriage, he devoted himself exclusively to song-writing. In 1841 he composed no fewer than three of his four great symphonies, and in 1842 his masterpieces of chamber music were produced.

In the beginning of this year he was induced to break through his retirement, and to accompany his wife on a concert tour to Hamburg, where his B flat Symphony was performed, and whence she went on to Copenhagen without him, since he preferred going back to his labours. In the summer of the same year they went for a tour in Bohemia, but he could not but be conscious that the divine afflatus was upon him, and that he must devote himself heart and soul to composition. In 1843 he wrote the cantata, "Paradise and the Peri," his first essay in the direction of concerted vocal music. And at this point, when his outward circumstances were of the happiest kind, when he had won the woman who of all others was the most capable of making him happy, he stood at the zenith of his career, having obtained absolute mastery over every form of music. At this point, therefore, we may most fitly close our examination of the second section of Robert Schumann's life, and the first of his artistic career.

CHAPTER III.

THE SHADOW OF DEATH.

1843—1856.

WE have seen how Schumann, after passing through
the many and various difficulties that beset him at the
beginning of his life, and again at the outset of his
professional career, had at length attained to the
fulfilment of all his desires. The art of composition
had now been perfectly mastered. No longer do we
hear of those early struggles to acquire the faculty of
casting his musical ideas into perfect form. He had
reached a point where composition came easily to him,
and henceforth in all that he writes we trace that
feeling of spontaneity which is the mark of all con-
summate achievements in art. His outward circumstances, as we have said, were entirely favourable to
his creative activity, and fortune seemed once again to
shine upon him. No doubt he would have been still
happier than he was if he had met with a little more
appreciation from his contemporaries and fellow-
musicians, for whom he himself had always a word of
praise whenever it could reasonably be bestowed. But
this want is one which he shares with all the greatest
men of the earth, or almost all. Since the day when
Cimabue's Madonna was enthroned in the church of

Santa Maria Novella amid the joyful acclamation of all Florence, it may be doubted whether any of the world's greatest men have ever received the universal homage of their contemporaries. This has been reserved for those of secondary achievement. And, indeed, so few have been the exceptions to the rule, that it may almost be held to be a test of true greatness that an artist, whether poet, painter, or musician, should be despised and rejected by those among whom he lives. As Landor says, " We cannot hope for both celebrity and fame : supremely fortunate are the few who are allowed the liberty of choice between them."

It is curious to reflect that all the honour which the world gave to Schumann during his life was the degree of Doctor at Jena, and a professorship in the conservatorium of Leipzig, which had been founded through the exertions of Mendelssohn, and to which Schumann was appointed on April 3rd, 1843. In the winter of the same year the first performance of " Paradise and the Peri " took place in the Gewandhaus, and the work so enthusiastically received that it had to be given again in a week's time. But successes like this were very few, and only served as the exceptions to the rule just given. Though his own triumphs were of the rarest occurrence, he could share in those of his wife, and we know that her successes were keenly enjoyed by him. In the spring of 1844 they went together on a concert tour to Russia, and in a letter written by Schumann from St. Petersburg to his father-in-law (with whom a reconciliation had been brought about in the previous year), we see that the journey gave him the greatest possible pleasure. The public triumphs of Madame Schumann, the great favour with which the two artists were received in the musical world of the Russian capital, and the frequent intercourse with Adolph Henselt, were the most important elements in Schumann's enjoyment.

On their return to Leipzig in June, he began to think of severing his connection with the *Neue Zeitschrift*, which had now lasted just ten years. Since 1840, the year in which he first attained to perfect freedom of musical expression, the direction of the journal had occupied a secondary place in his thoughts, and the want of success which attended his endeavours to publish it in Vienna probably conduced to his intention of giving up the regular work of the paper. After July, 1844, he was only an occasional contributor. In addition to his composition there were duties in connection with the professorship, of which we have spoken; and to these he now applied himself. But it does not appear that he had any of the special gifts which go to make a good teacher. He seems to have lacked the power of imparting instruction in words, and of communicating to the pupil the method by which any desired effect was to be obtained. His biographer, Wasielewski, gives from his personal recollection a very good instance of his peculiarities of tuition He tells us that he (the writer) had to play the violin part in the B flat trio of Schubert in one of the classes for concerted music, and that Schumann scarcely opened his lips, during the whole lesson, although, as Wasielewski modestly admits, there was plenty of opportunity for correction. The habits of silence and reserve, which were growing upon him more and more, were no doubt signs of the progress of that mental affliction which from this time onwards increased with every year, the attacks of nervous excitement and unaccountable melancholy becoming more and more frequent as time went on. The state of his health was no doubt the principal reason for his move to Dresden, which took place in October of this year. It was thought, and probably with some truth, that he had suffered from too much music in Leipzig, and that in a new atmosphere he might recover from the weariness and lassitude which oppressed him, and in time regain some of the musical ardour of his earlier life. His position in Leipzig obliged him to hear an immense amount of music, and in Dresden he need only hear what he liked. The relief that he felt at first is expressed in a letter to F. David, in which he says, "Here" (in Dresden) "one can get back the old lost longing for music, there is so little to hear! It just suits my condition, for I still suffer very much from my nerves, and everything affects and exhausts me directly."

Though Leipzig ceased to be his home from the autumn of 1844, it was not till December of that year that he settled for good in Dresden, after having taken his farewell of Leipzig at a *matinée musicale* on December 8th. We must not infer from his relief at hearing less music that he had become negligent as far as his own compositions were concerned. During this very time we know that he was working far too intensely at the "Scenes from Faust." A Dresden doctor, named Helbig, strongly recommended him to distract his thoughts and to take up some interest altogether apart from music, but this he could by no means be persuaded to do. Dr. Helbig's account of Schumann's physical and mental condition is quoted by Wasielewski, and is of course most interesting, since it gives an exact description of the symptoms of the case, and its peculiar circumstances. Of these the most remarkable were that he lost the power of remembering musical ideas, even when he was composing, and that he was constantly troubled with what may be called an auricular delusion, imagining that he heard one particular note (an A) always going on. This state of things lasted with slight intermissions until February, 1846, when he regained much of his former health, both in mind and body; not that the clouds which had gathered thickly around him were ever again dispersed altogether, but before the final darkness they parted, for intervals of longer or shorter duration. When we consider the grandeur and breadth of the works which were produced during the years between his residence in Dresden and his death, it is almost impossible to believe them to be the compositions of one who laboured under so severe an affliction as that to which Schumann was subject. For a long time he seems to have possessed the power of resisting, so far as music was concerned, the influence of his disease, and it was only in his relations with others, and apart from music, that his condition was seen at its worst. The silence and depression by which he had for a long time been affected, were now almost unconquerable, even by his most intimate friends. It is true that during the years he spent at Dresden he became very fond of Fer-

dinand Hiller, and that he interested himself considerably in Richard Wagner, who was at that time in
Dresden. His opinion of " Tannhäuser," which was not
very favourable at first, became gradually more and
more so; and from this it is evident that he retained
sufficient energy and perseverance to devote time and
attention to the study of such a work as this.

With the improvement in his health came the determination to perfect himself in a branch of musical
science to which he thought he had not given enough
time, viz., counterpoint. The result of his ardour is
comprised in the works for the pedal-piano, all of
which show more contrapuntal skill than had appeared
in any earlier compositions. Among the greater
works, most of the pianoforte concerto and the C major
Symphony date from this period (1845-46); and certainly no music could be more free from all trace of
morbid feeling than these two masterpieces of Schumann's art.

In the winter of 1846-47 the Schumanns visited
Vienna, and stayed there several weeks. Madame
Schumann gave some concerts, and in the early part
of the year they returned by way of Prague, where two
concerts were given, at one of which the pianoforte
quintet was played with the greatest success. In the
summer they went for a short time to Zwickau, and
Schumann had the satisfaction of a really enthusiastic
reception in his native town. The new symphony and
the pianoforte concerto were performed under Schu
mann's direction, and were highly appreciated.

The good effects produced by these journeys on
Schumann's health may be traced in the list of works

composed in this year, which is more than usually ex-
tensive. Two trios for piano and strings, and a considerable amount of vocal music, both for solos and
chorus, were written, and a great part of one of his
chief works, the opera of "Genoveva," was planned,
though little was actually composed except the overture. The realization of one of his most cherished
schemes was at hand. It appears that as early as 1840
he had begun to think about writing a grand opera;
but his purpose did not become fixed till 1844 or
thereabouts, when he commenced to cast about in good
earnest for a libretto, or rather for a subject that would
attract his imagination and inspire his creative powers.
Among the many subjects that suggested themselves,
the following are the most worthy of note : " Faust,"
the "Nibelungenlied," the " Wartburg Tournament of
Song," and the " Veiled Prophet " from Moore's " Lalla
Rookh." The first of these ideas was used, as we have
seen, in a different way, in the form of the " Scenes from
Goethe's ' Faust ; ' " and it seems very probable that the
last would have been chosen, but for the fact that an
Oriental subject had quite recently been set by him,
which, moreover, was taken from the same English poem.
He intended to turn his attention to this subject at a
later date, and it is evident from a letter on the subject
to Zuccalmaglio that he was quite aware of the dramatic capabilities of Moore's story. It was not till
many years after Schumann's death that an opera was
written upon the " Veiled Prophet " by Mr. C. Villiers
Stanford, one of the most ardent of Schumann's
admirers. The third of the stories we have mentioned
had been appropriated by Wagner before Schumann

had begun even the outline of his own work, and therefore was out of the question.   It is just possible, too,
that the idea of giving musical treatment to the " Nibelungenlied " may have occurred to Wagner as early
as this, though the four poems which make up " Der
Ring des Nibelungen " were not written till 1853.
However this may be, it is in vain to wish that we had
two musical settings of the great Norse myth, and by
two such different men as Wagner and Schumann.

At last, in the beginning of 1847, Schumann became
acquainted with Hebbel's play on the story of
" Geneviève," and at once decided to adopt the subject
for his opera.   He wished to temper the harrowing
and sensational scenes of that drama by infusing into
the libretto some of the spirit of Tieck's poem on the
same subject, but his efforts to get a satisfactory
book made by Robert Reinick were unsuccessful, and
Hebbel himself could not be induced to modify his
work to please Schumann.   He was obliged therefore
to compile a libretto for himself from the two works
and as best he could, and it must be confessed that
the result is by no means altogether successful.
The words will be spoken of more fully when we
come to consider the opera as a whole.

In the beginning of 1848 we find Schumann in a
much more satisfactory condition than he had been
for some time.   The last touches were given to the
" Scenes from ' Faust,' " and the opera was approaching completion.   He now succeeded his friend Hiller
as conductor of a choral society for male voices.
This occupation gave him a new interest, and the
work happened at this time to be particularly con-

genial to him, as he had lately composed several choral works for men's voices, and an opportunity was afforded him of hearing the effect of some of the "Faust" choruses.

In this, the later part of his residence in Dresden, it is curious to notice that, whereas he had always been used to take up one form of musical composition with great energy at one time, and to devote himself exclusively to it while the mood was on him, he now produced works in almost every form; vocal music and instrumental, chamber music and orchestral, works of large and of small calibre, were produced with the greatest possible rapidity. His compositions seemed, as it were, to flow in an irresistible stream, nor could the interruptions caused by outward circumstances deter him from his work. The list for 1849 is larger and more varied than that for any other year; but at the same time it contains fewer of those works which have been accepted as his finest. The best work of this period is the "Manfred" music.

Schumann left Dresden for a time in 1849, when that disturbance took place in which Richard Wagner, who in politics as in art was an ardent revolutionary, bore no inconsiderable part. Schumann's nature unfitted him utterly for public life in any form, and we may feel sure that the sensitive composer, with his reserved, silent disposition, would have made a very poor demagogue indeed, even if he had held the extreme views of his younger brother in art. He seems to have been sufficiently in sympathy with the insurrectionists to make his stay at Dresden somewhat undesirable, and in the little village of Kreischa, about four and a half miles off, he could go on peacefully with his work, and yet be within hearing of the stirring events of that month of May.

In the midst of this turbulent state of affairs, Schumann heard of a new sphere of work for which he considered himself fitted by his signal success in conducting the chorus of male voices, of which mention has been already made. On the death of Mendelssohn, Julius Rietz had succeeded to the post of conductor at the Gewandhaus in Leipzig, and rumour now said that Rietz was appointed Capellmeister at Berlin. Thereupon Schumann caused application to be made for the post at the Gewandhaus through a certain Dr. Härtel. The endeavour to obtain the appointment was unsuccessful, since Rietz was not removed from Leipzig. It seems pretty certain that the post would not have been well filled if Schumann had been appointed, for the same qualities which prevented his being a good teacher stood in his way as a conductor. It is related that his constitutional diffidence of manner was so strong that he could not bring himself to correct his orchestra for any particular mistake, or to draw attention to it, but would simply direct them to begin again at the beginning. If the band did not discover the mistake for themselves, it had to remain uncorrected at the performance.

In August, 1849, the one hundredth anniversary of Goethe's birth gave occasion for the performance of the "Scenes from 'Faust,'" and accordingly such of these as were by this time completed were given, together with Mendelssohn's "Walpurgisnacht," both at Dresden and Leipzig, Schumann's work alone being performed at the same time at Weimar. The " Scenes," as we now have them, were not finished until 1853, and were not published till after the composer's death.

Schumann's wish for the Gewandhaus post had left him the desire for some kind of regular duty connected with music, and accordingly, during the winter of 1849-50, we find him making arrangements in order to obtain some such post as that which he had wished for at Leipzig. Some influential friends in Dresden tried to get for him an appointment as assistant Capell-meister there, but from some cause or other this also fell through. While he was in doubt about this, how-ever, a much better post was actually offered to him: a vacancy of a similar kind had occurred at Düssel-dorf in consequence of Ferdinand Hiller's removal to Cologne. The only drawback, or at all events the chief one, to the new post, was the distance of Düssel-dorf from the neighbourhood where Schumann had lived all his life; but after some preliminary negotiations had been settled—Hiller himself being the medium of communication throughout—Schumann decided to accept the offer. Before taking up his abode in Düsseldorf he had to fulfil several engagements; of these the most important was the superintendence of the production of " Genoveva " in Leipzig.

In the early spring of the year he undertook another concert tour with his wife, visiting Leipzig, Bremen, and Hamburg. From a letter written by Madame Schumann to Hiller, we hear of four weeks pleasantly spent in Leipzig, and in Hamburg she says that Jenny Lind had sung at the two final concerts of the tour,

so that the success of the undertaking is manifest.
The preparations for "Genoveva" were later in the
year, as the opera was produced on June 25, and for
this event the Schumanns again went to Leipzig. The
time of year was unpropitious, and the work did not
suit the taste of the Leipzig public; at all events, it
was received without much enthusiasm. The warmest
admirer of the new work seems to have been Spohr,
who was unfeignedly delighted with it.

The move to Düsseldorf was not made until September, 1850, and his first appearance as conductor took
place on October 24th. In his new capacity of musical
director (Städtischer Musikdirector) he had to conduct
not only an orchestra, but also a vocal union. A series
of concerts of the most successful kind was given
during the winter, and at the first some of his own
works were performed, under the direction of Julius
Tausch. The new sphere of action contained all that
he could desire—regular work, a good orchestra and
chorus at command, always ready to perform his
new compositions as soon as they were written, and
the power of bringing to a hearing whatsoever music
he considered worthy of that honour. Now at last he
was in a position to hold out to young composers the
encouragement he had always wished to give them. We
know from many passages in his writings how dear to
his heart was the cause of young musical aspirants, and
we need not wonder when we find that during his first
concert season in Düsseldorf one of the evenings was
devoted exclusively to the works of living composers,
a proceeding at that time quite unheard of.

In connection with this change of residence there

appears for the first time a curious peculiarity, which proves to be a foreshadowing of presentiment of the fate which was now so near. In one of the letters to Hiller which bear upon the subject of the Düsseldorf appointment, he expresses his horror at finding that the town contained a lunatic asylum; he describes how he had once or twice stayed in a house whose windows looked out upon an institution of the sort, and how the constant sight of it had preyed upon his mind. He takes comfort, however, from the idea that after all his information may have been incorrect, and that the asylum may turn out to be nothing more gloomy than a hospital. From the way in which he is able to reason himself out of his nervous dread, we see that at the time this letter was written he was in an unusually satisfactory condition, and one altogether the reverse of morbid. The influence of Dresden, and the interest he took in public matters at this time, had no doubt been good, and had taken him out of himself for the time being. This more hopeful condition of things was not of long duration, though at first Schumann seemed to have received much benefit from the change of life as well as the change of scene. His creative facility was greater than ever. The " Rhine Symphony " and a number of ballads set elaborately and at considerable length, of which the " Pilgrimage of the Rose " is the most prominent, were the most important of the works produced during the early part of the Düsseldorf period. Besides these, there are many isolated compositions of almost every kind, and we hear of schemes for a second opera and for an oratorio. Neither of these came to anything, but the last project

D

bore fruit in a Mass and a Requiem. The only permanent result of the operatic scheme was the composition of an overture to Schiller's "Braut von Messina," in which play he had been much interested, with a view to having an opera libretto written upon it.

A journey to Switzerland with his family in the summer of 1851, a short visit to Antwerp in August of the same year, in order to act as judge at a competition of the Belgian " Männergesangverein," and a week spent in Leipzig in March, 1852, broke what by this time had become the monotonous routine of the life at Düsseldorf. The Leipzig visit was fully occupied with the performances of Schumann's own music; to such a point had his fame increased even in that cold and unappreciative town.

The Lower Rhine Music Festival (Niederrheinische Musikfest) is the largest and most celebrated institution of the kind in Germany. It is held at Whitsuntide in annual rotation at Cologne, Aix, and Düsseldorf, so that in each town it is usually of triennial recurrence, like our own provincial festivals. In May, 1853, the thirty-first of these gatherings took place at Düsseldorf, and in ordinary circumstances the task of directing the entire festival would have devolved on Schumann. He, however, only conducted the music on the first day, consisting of Handel's " Messiah " and his own symphony in D minor; the rest of the festival was conducted by Hiller, at Schumann's request. It had grown of late more and more evident that Schumann's powers of conducting were not adequate to such a task as was now set before them; and symptoms of failing health had begun once again to show themselves. No doubt the regularity of the work at Düsseldorf, that very regularity which he had thought would be so greatly beneficial, had begun to have no good effect on him. If in earlier life he had had some similar post, he might very probably not have felt his present duties to be injurious, but his strength was now not sufficient for all that he had to do; and, besides, the consciousness of his shortcomings as a conductor, which he, with his sensitive nature, cannot but have felt, must have added not a little to the irksomeness of his position. When we know that one of the most marked signs of the mental disorder which was now beginning to show itself, was that all music heard by him seemed to be taken too fast, and that accordingly he slackened the pace of every composition which he himself conducted,[1] there is little difficulty in accounting for the desire on the part of the authorities to procure a substitute for him. They wished very naturally to effect this without hurting Schumann's feelings, and an attempt was made after the first concert of the winter series in 1853 to induce him to retire, but Schumann felt aggrieved by their well-meant insinuations, and the result was a difference of no amicable kind. Julius Tausch, of whom mention has before been made, succeeded him as conductor, and Schumann began to take measures for a speedy departure from Düsseldorf. His thoughts turned once more to Vienna, as they had done on a former occasion, but

[1] On one occasion, when he was conducting a symphony of his own, he continued to beat time after the conclusion of the work, oblivious of the fact that the players had stopped.

his wish to live there was not destined to be fulfilled.

The annoyance caused by this misunderstanding
with the authorities was in some degree counter-
balanced by a very great pleasure which came to
Schumann in the same month as that first concert of
the series, after which, as we have said, he laid down
the conductor's bâton. A letter of introduction was
brought to Schumann from Joseph Joachim, recommending to his notice a young composer of whose
powers the writer had formed the highest opinion. The
bearer of the letter was no other than Johannes Brahms,
and the reception which he got from Schumann, as
soon as his works had been seen, must have far ex-
ceeded the most sanguine hopes of the aspiring composer. At once Schumann recognized the surpassing
capabilities of the young man, and wrote to Joachim
these words, and nothing more: " Das ist der, der
kommen musste " ("This is he who was wanted to
come "). In defence of his new friend's qualifications
as a composer, Schumann returned for the last time into
the world of letters, and published in the periodical
with which he had been so intimately connected an
article entitled " New Paths " ("Neue Bahnen "),
which is certainly one of his most remarkable writings.
In it Schumann seems to sing his " Nunc Dimittis,"
hailing the advent of this young and ardent spirit, who
was to carry on the line of great composers, and to
prove himself no unworthy member of their glorious
company. The concluding sentence of the article,
which contained the composer's last printed words, is
not a little remarkable, for it gives fullest expression

to that principle which had always governed his own criticisms, and which is in the highest degree valuable for all criticism : "In every age there is a secret band of kindred spirits. Ye who are of this fellowship, see that ye weld the circle firmly, that so the truth of Art may shine ever more and more clearly, shedding joy and blessing far and near."

Little more remains to be told. In the winter of 1853 a concert tour was undertaken by the Schumanns in Holland, and the reception there accorded to his music, more especially at Utrecht and Rotterdam, gave him the keenest satisfaction. In January, 1854, " Paradise and the Peri " was performed at Hanover, and while there Schumann had some pleasant intercourse with several congenial spirits. On his return he took considerable interest in preparing his critical and other writings for the press, and even contemplated a new literary scheme. Very soon after this journey, however, his mental condition assumed the gravest aspect, and he became a prey to almost unintermittent melancholy. Beside the old delusion of a persistent musical note always audible, there appear to have been hallucinations of a more vivid kind. On one occasion he was under the impression that Schubert and Mendelssohn had visited him and had given him a musical theme, which he wrote down, and upon which he set himself to write variations. These were never finished, but it is not a little curious that almost immediately after the tragic circumstance which compelled his friends to place him under medical restraint, he resumed the task of composing on this same theme with renewed energy. Schumann's own variations have never been published,

but the theme which originated in so curious a manner
has been used by Brahms for a set of four-hand variations, and published as his op. 23.   The terrible
disease had not given any manifestations of an alarming
kind, but on February 27th, 1854, in one of his more
acute attacks of melancholy, he attempted to commit
suicide by throwing himself into the Rhine. He was
saved by some boatmen and restored to his friends.
After this it was of course necessary to place him under
restraint, and indeed he himself had expressed his will-
ingness to be confined in an asylum, even before this
sad event.   He was placed under the care of Dr.
Richarz, who had a private asylum at Endenich, near
Bonn, and here he remained for two years, his condition
showing occasional improvement, so that he was not
debarred altogether from intercourse with his friends.
A touching account of his condition at this time is given
by his biographer, Wasielewski, who visited him in the
summer of 1855, and was allowed to watch him un-
observed as he sat at his piano improvising. The end
came on July 29th, 1856. He died at four o'clock in
the afternoon, in the presence of his beloved wife, and
was buried two days afterwards at Bonn, in the church-
yard opposite the Sternenthor.

Seventeen years after the master's death, a festival
in his honour was held in the town where he was
interred. This took place on August 17th, 18th,
and 19th, 1873, and was devoted entirely to Schumann's works. Of these nearly all the most remarkable were performed; his widow, his biographer
Wasielewski, and Joachim, taking an active part in
the arrangements. The proceeds were used for the

erection of a monument above the composer's grave, and this was unveiled in 1880, when a concert of great interest was given.

Those who knew Schumann well describe him as a man of moderately tall stature, well-built, and of a dignified and pleasant aspect. The outlines of his face, with its intellectual brow, and its lower part inclining slightly to heaviness, are sufficiently familiar to us all; but we cannot see the dreamy, half-shut eyes kindle into animation at a word from some friend with whom he felt himself in sympathy, nor have we any sketch or drawing which would show us what he looked like in ordinary life, or when engaged in earnest conversation with his friends. In the case of Beethoven there exists a most valuable sketch, if sketch it should be called, and not rather caricature, which gives us an impression of the man such as no other portrait can convey; but with Schumann there is nothing of the kind, or if there be, it has never been published. We have to content ourselves with verbal descriptions.

We have seen that, so far as outward circumstances were concerned, Schumann's life was uneventful; the crises through which he passed were nearly all of a mental kind, but perhaps for that very reason they were the more trying, seeing that in the greater number he could apply to no friend for sympathy or counsel. Until his marriage he was almost entirely debarred, partly, no doubt, by his own reticence, from the closest intimacy even with those to whom he was most attached; and we can hardly doubt that, forced as he was to live a life of spiritual loneliness, his constitutional habit of melancholy, and his inherent tendency towards insanity had a more fatal effect upon him than they would have had if he had persuaded himself to seek the sympathy of those around him more diligently, and to have opened his heart more freely to those by whom he was beloved.

CHAPTER IV.

THE PIANOFORTE WORKS.

AT the outset of any account of Robert Schumann's compositions, one group of works must command chief, and, for a time, exclusive attention. We have seen that it was his practice to confine himself almost entirely to one class of composition at a time, and that he never rested, or turned his attention to another branch of the art, until he had done the best he could in the particular class he had chosen. Since at the beginning of his artistic career he intended to fit himself for the profession of a pianist, it is easy to account for the fact that his earliest compositions are one and all for the instrument which it was his ambition to play. It is not often easy, and in many cases it is quite impossible, to trace the course of an artist's growth from his published works; but in Schumann's pianoforte compositions we are permitted to watch his gradual development, and to see how the mysteries of musical form became ever more and more clear to his understanding. At first he wisely refrained from attempting to write in the classical form at all, and it was not till the sixth year from the time of his beginning composition that he wrote his first sonata; but there is no evidence that he was hampered in the ex-

pression of his ideas by his lack of theoretical musical
knowledge. He had found a form which met all the
requirements of his creative faculty, and in which he
could express all that he wished. This form, if form
it can indeed be called, consists in the combination of
many short musical organisms into one set or collection
of pieces, the whole becoming organic by means of the
inherent connection between the component parts. All
Schumann's most important compositions for the piano,
as well as many of those which are less remarkable,
are in this form, though it is curious that he seldom, if
ever, uses it for works of any other kind. Many of
the songs, indeed, are in sets, as the "Dichterliebe,"
" Frauenliebe," &c. But the form is not the same, for
any song may be sung by itself without losing any of
its beauty or significance, while in the case of the
pianoforte works, no piece can be taken out of its
surroundings without some detriment to its proper
effect.

Before considering the most important and the best
known of the piano works, we must take a cursory
glance at the earliest efforts of the composer. The
" Abegg" variations (op. 1) originated, as has been
already related, in Schumann's having met at a ball at
Mannheim a young lady named Meta Abegg. He experienced towards her just so much of the gentle passion as warranted him in turning her name into a
musical phrase, and writing a set of variations on a
melody constructed upon that phrase. The work is
not musically of any importance, and the influence of
Moscheles is evident throughout; but it is highly
interesting to the pianoforte student, for it shows how

deeply its author had penetrated into the techniquᵥ of the instrument, and even in this first composition there is, in the finale, an instance of an effect of Schumann's own invention, viz., the gradual taking off of a chord from the bass upwards, leaving at last the uppermost note sounding alone. The published variations appeared with a dedication to a purely imaginary " Pauline, Comtesse d'Abegg."

It was about the same time that Schumann heard Paganini, and that his admiration found expression in a transcription of six of his caprices for the piano (op. 3). The chief interest attaching to this production is due to the preface, in which Schumann explains the purpose of the work, and gives many directions of the highest possible value, concerning the proper style of rendering to be adopted in these and similar pieces. Some time after the publication of the first set of caprice-studies, a second set (op. 10) was undertaken. These have much greater intrinsic value than the earlier series, for the composer no longer adheres religiously to the actual notes of Paganini, but allows his own individuality to appear, enriching and extending Paganini's themes with great success.

We now have to consider the first of those sets or cycles of pieces of which passing mention was made above. The " Papillons " (op. 2) are a genuine " Jean-Pauliad," to use Schumann's own expression. The title was no doubt meant to embody all sorts of fanciful ideas, such as the upward soaring of his genius when freed from the bondage of its chrysalis condition, by which last figure he would represent the long period of his legal studies, before he was allowed to look for-

ward to the musician's career. There appears not to be
any intimate connection between the title and the pieces
themselves. The meaning of these, as the composer
himself tells us in a letter to Henriette Voigt, is to be
found in the last chapter—or rather the last but one
—of Jean Paul's " Flegeljahre," in which a ball is
described. Beyond its youthful freshness and its
constant variety, the work as a whole has no very
great importance, nor can it compare for a moment
with the " Carnaval," for which it undoubtedly
served as the sketch (conf. the two finales, and the
way in which No. 1 of the " Papillons " recurs in
" Florestan " of the " Carnaval "). Yet there are in
the earlier work individual pieces of extraordinary
charm, such as Nos. 1, 4, 5, 7, and 10. No. 8 was
once made the vehicle of a joke by its composer, who
passed it off upon his friend Töpken as a waltz by
Schubert. No. 9 is also interesting as containing in
its second section the germ of a phrase that was used
by Schumann in several later works. This beautiful
effect of a scale with one or more chromatic intervals,
rising persistently under, through, and above the rest
of the parts, which are as persistently stationary,
whether the notes are sustained or repeated, occurs
again in the first movement of the quintett, in the
slow movement of the trio in F (op. 80), and in the
first of the " Fantasie-Stücke," for piano alone.

Although some of the other cycles of pianoforte pieces
come considerably later in order of publication, yet they
were nearly all written in this first period of Schumann's career as a composer, so that it will be most convenient to examine them in this place.   In those cycles

which are best known, the " Carnaval," the " Fantasie-Stücke," the " Kinderscenen," and the " Waldscenen," all the pieces have some title or other, as the name of a person or a character, of an incident or a scene. Though these are, one and all, felt to be absolutely true as musical delineations, and as representing individualities of character or incident in a way that is far beyond the power of words, it must not be supposed that the composer deliberately set himself, as some maker of drawing-room pieces might do now-a-days, to write a musical description of such an individual or such a scene. In every case, as Schumann himself tells us, the piece was written first, and the right name found for it afterwards. He viewed the other method with supreme contempt. Whatever his manner of working, there is no doubt that he possessed the most extra-ordinary power of perceiving and giving musical ex-pression to the salient points in a character or circum-stance that took his fancy. The reader will remember how he used to amuse himself and his schoolfellows in a way very like this.

In the " Six Intermezzi " (op. 4) we have a set of pieces to the meaning of which the author has given us no clue, except in the middle section of No. 2, where the words " Meine Ruh' ist hin " may perhaps be taken as an indication that the whole number is to be under-stood as a delineation of Goethe's " Gretchen " as she appears in the later scenes of " Faust," Part I. With the exception of No. 4, all the Intermezzos are in the same form, a modification of the *da-capo* form, the middle section of each being called " Alternativo," after which the first subject returns. They are highly

interesting, in a purely musical point of view, though
their fame has been eclipsed by that of the "Novelletten," which, like them, are left unexplained by the
composer, and to which they stand in the same
relation that the "Papillons" do to the "Carnaval."

Of all the pianoforte works, the "Carnaval" (op. 9)
is perhaps the most popular; its wonderful animation
and never-ending variety ensure the production of its
full effect, and its great and various difficulties make it
the best possible test of a pianist's skill and versatility.
The theme of the whole composition is a phrase of the
most unpromising character, consisting of the four
notes A, E flat, C and B — called in German A, S, C, H
which thus make up the name of the town where
Schumann's friend, Ernestine von Fricken, lived. The
name is also translated into musical notes in another
way, as A flat, C and B, A flat being called As in
German. It happens, too, that these four letters are
the only letters in the name Schumann which bear a
musical significance. The three phrases thus generated
are given in their simplest form in the number called
"Sphinxes." In the entire collection of pieces there
are only two that contain no reference to these notes
and by far the greater number are actually developed
from them. And yet not even Schumann ever wrote
a work in which there was more constant variety, or
one in which the delineation of characters, both real
and imaginary, was more true to nature. The members
of the mystic "Davidsbund" jostle with the four
time-honoured figures of pantomime. There are also
four portrait-studies, labelled respectively "Chiarina,"
"Chopin," "Paganini," and "Estrelle," of which the

first three are such speaking likenesses—" Chiarina "
is a portrait of Madame Schumann at the age of
fifteen—that we feel absolutely certain that " Estrelle "
is no less perfect a presentment of the fair Ernestine,
and that we know her as thoroughly as if we had seen
her in the flesh. Among the prettiest numbers are
three called " Reconnaissance," " Aveu," and " Pro-
menade," which may be regarded as making up the
description of some tender episode. The finale is that
wonderful " Marche des Davidsbündler contre les
Philistius," in which the fatuous old tune of the
' Grossvatertanz " is used to represent the enemies
of musical enlightenment, and is worried, laughed at,
attacked, and at last thrust ignominiously from the
scene.

A work which is no less masterly in design and
effective in execution dates from the same year as the
" Carnaval," and, like it, is built upon a theme connected with Schumann's brief affection for Mdlle. von
Fricken. The melody on which the " Études Symphoniques " (op. 13) are written is from the pen of the
lady's father, and a very beautiful melody it is. All
the studies or variations, as they are indifferently called,
are instinct with originality and strength, and are full
of fancy; some of them, as for instance No. 2, and the
variation immediately preceding the finale, rise to a
height of passion that had not been attained in any
former work of Schumann's. The whole concludes
with a brilliant movement developed at considerable
length, in which the theme of the variations appears
only in a subordinate position; the opening subject is
taken from a song in Marschner's opera " Templer

und Jüdin," which contains the words "Du stolzes England, freue dich." The adoption of this theme for the finale was intended by Schumann as a compliment to Sterndale Bennett, who had just come to Leipzig at the time when the variations were composed, and to whom Schumann dedicated them. It is to be feared that the English composer scarcely estimated the honour that Schumann had done him at its true value, for it is related that on one occasion, in after-years, he heard the work played, and failed to recognize it.

It was not till 1835 that any attempt to use the sonata-form was made. The only two works which are actually called sonatas date from this year. The first (op. 11), in F sharp minor, is remarkable as being the only composition actually published under a pseudonym by Schumann. Its original title runs—" Sonata for the pianoforte, dedicated to Clara by Florestan and Eusebius." No more accurate description of the contents of the sonata could be given than that which is conveyed in the title. The two contrasting sides of the composer's character are brought out in strongest relief, nor is there throughout any attempt at compromise or coalition between them. Eusebius leads off with an Adagio of great beauty and of a more passionate character than most of the music to which his name is applied. This introduces the first movement proper, in which the restless and impulsive Florestan reigns supreme. This movement, like the finale, in which the same side of the author's character is brought out, is developed at great length, but is singularly deficient in proportion and beauty of structure, though individual

passages here and there have a considerable degree
of charm and originality. The best section of the
sonata is the slow movement, and it is at the same
time the simplest and most unpretentious. The
scherzo is very good, and it also contains a genuine
piece of musical fun in the burlesque pomposity of the
Intermezzo, and in the turgid piece of mock-heroic
recitative that leads back to the scherzo.

The second sonata (op. 22), in G minor, had been
begun as early as 1833, and was not finished in its
ultimate form until 1838. A great advance is perceptible, in respect of clearness of expression, in both
the first and last movements. The time-directions in
the first movement are sufficiently amusing ; the
opening is marked " Il più presto possibile," and yet at
the end the player is told to increase the pace, the
words " più mosso " occurring at the beginning of the
coda, and "ancora più animato" twenty-five bars
before the close.

The Fantasia in C (op. 17), dedicated to Liszt, deserves
to be mentioned in this place, for though it is very far
from conforming to the rules of sonata structure, it is
at least as good a sonata as that in F sharp minor.
There is certainly one particular in which it trans-
gresses the most elementary of the rules, viz., that the
slow movement is placed last of all. Though in the
present form of the work this arrangement is unexplained, we can understand it better when we know
the original purpose for which it was written. In
1835 a movement was set on foot throughout Germany
to raise a monument to Beethoven in his native town
of Bonn. Schumann's opinions concerning this project

E

may be read in four articles called "Beethoven's Monument," which are signed respectively by Florestan, Jonathan, Eusebius, and Raro. He conceived the plan of contributing, not a sum of money, but a musical composition, of which the pecuniary proceeds should be given to the fund. What is now known as the Fantasia in C is that composition; its title was to have been "Obolus," as a modest indication of its purpose; and the three movements were to be called "Ruins," "Triumphal Arch," and "The Starry Crown" (Ruinen, Triumphbogen, and Sternenkranz). For some reason or other the work was not published at this time, and it was afterwards altered in name, and the motto from Schlegel added, as we now have it. In point of form, an advance has again been made, for all the departures from the orthodox sonata structure are intentional, and not merely the result of insufficient knowledge or study; and in respect of its noble themes, its spontaneity, and its depth of passion, it takes very high rank among the piano works of Schumann.

The sonata in F minor (op. 14), was, when first published, called, in deference to a foolish whim of the publisher, "Concert pour pianoforte seul." In order that the title should not be quite inappropriate Schumann made certain modifications in the first movement, and left out the two scherzos. In the second edition of the work he restored the first movement to its original form, and put in one of the scherzos. The sonata is of great beauty throughout; it is scarcely less imaginative than the Fantasia of which we have just spoken, and in point of form it is much better. The slow movement consists of variations on a theme by Clara Wieck, which are treated in Schumann's happiest vein. The finale is most interesting, although a little too long.

Beside the defects in technical form, there is one fault which is common to all the sonatas, and that is an entire lack of real unity between the movements, and it is all the more remarkable because in after-life no quality is more prominent in all the composer's concerted and orchestral compositions, than this same unity, the want of which is so deeply felt in his early attempts. But yet, with all their departures from precedent and real defects, the beauties which these works contain must endear them to every lover of music, as well as to every student of Schumann's compositions.

The next group of works which we have to consider is of the highest interest, for, as he himself admits, most, if not all of them, bear the reflection of his emotional state in one of the most critical periods of his life,—those years, namely, during which he strove so valiantly for the hand of Clara Wieck. The four years of suspense and anxiety bore the richest fruit in the shape of compositions which for vividness of imagination, and truth of spiritual portraiture, have never been surpassed. In point of form, a return is made to the old "cyclic" arrangement; the individual pieces are longer and more elaborately treated than is the case in the earlier works, and as a rule they can be played separately, and are so intended by the composer. The practice of affixing names to the separate pieces is gradually discarded, and where they are given, we cannot but feel in some instances that the whole meaning is in no wise expressed by the name. In the " Fantasiestücke " (op. 12) some of the names are quite indefinite, and we are free to imagine the composer's intention for ourselves. In the " Kinderscenen " (op. 15) all the titles are definite except the last one, which may be taken as containing the moral of the whole. " The poet speaks " to those for whom he has conjured up scenes from their own childhood, and delivers himself of the *envoi* of his poem. We may observe that this is the last work, dating from the period when he wrote exclusively for the piano, that is furnished with titles for the separate pieces.

The " Davidsbündler " (op. 6), to which title the name of " Dances " was at first appended, are not, as some have supposed, to be viewed as an extension of the finale of the " Carnaval," but as a development of the primary ideas represented by the names Florestan and Eusebius. The two contrasting characters appear here for the last time in music—the work, though called op. 6, was not composed till 1837—each piece being signed with one or other of their initials and some with both. A musical phrase of Clara Wieck's composition is prefixed to the whole as motto. To her both this work and the " Fantasiestücke " were sent from Vienna, and from letters which accompanied them, we see that they were mystic love-poems, meant to be completely intelligible only to her to whom they were sent. Exquisite as are some of the passages in the " Davidsbündler," some of the numbers are so wild and obscure that the work has never attained to a wide popularity.

The "Novelletten" (op. 21), the full meaning of which has never been disclosed, are intrinsically so beautiful, that they are much better known than any of the works in the group we are now examining; we know that there is an intention in them beyond their musical value, but we are given no clue except in the Intermezzo of the third number, which once bore the inscription from *Macbeth*, "When shall we three meet again," &c. These pieces, like the "Nachtstücke" (op. 23) and the "Humoreske" (op. 20), both of which were written in the year after the "Novelletten," appeal most definitely to the imagination of every musician, though the ideas which they call up are not in words to be expressed. The "Humoreske" differs only apparently in form from the others. It is really in the cyclic form, but the component parts are joined more closely together than is the case with the rest.

From the name "Kreisleriana" (op. 16), which is taken from the title of one of Hoffmann's "Fantasiestücke in Callots Manier," we might suppose that Schumann had returned to his early practice of transcribing in music the impression produced upon him by what he read, but in this instance a deeper meaning is to be perceived; under the guise of Hoffmann's quaint creation, the "Capellmeister Kreisler," there can be little doubt that Schumann means to present another portrait of himself, as he had done before in the "Davidsbündler." Florestan and Eusebius are not introduced in person, but it is easy to recognize their presence. The names were never used by Schumann in his music after the "Davidsbündler" (1837), and it was not long before they also disappeared from his prose writings, Eusebius making his last appearance in 1839, and Florestan in 1842. Thus the period during which this fancy was kept up, or what is called by one of the latest of Schumann's biographers his "Davidsbündlerperiode," corresponds almost exactly to that division of his life immediately preceding his marriage in which he devoted himself entirely to pianoforte composition. With a passing mention of some exceedingly graceful pieces of lighter structure— "Arabeske" (op. 18), "Blumenstück" (op. 19), "Scherzo, Gigue, Romanza, and Fughetta" (op. 32), by name—we come to one which is of great interest, since it reflects most definitely the impression produced upon the composer by his first visit to Vienna, when he went there in 1838 with the intention of bringing out the *Neue Zeitschrift* in that city. The "Faschingsschwank aus Wien"—carnival jest from Vienna—consists of four movements, of which three are among the brightest and most attractive creations of the composer. The point of the joke lies in the first movement, in which the "Marseillaise," a tune at that time interdicted in Vienna, is surreptitiously introduced. It is surely not too fanciful to interpret the second movement, Romance, as a representation of Schumann's weariness and disappointment in the gay Austrian capital, concerning which, as we have seen, his hopes had been so sanguine.

The piano works written after 1839 are so few and comparatively so unimportant that they may be noticed in a very few words. Among the solos, the "Waldscenen" (op. 82), the four marches (op. 76), and the

mysterious " Morning Songs " (op. 133), the last composition of the master, written during the sad final
years of his life, are the most prominent. The collec-
tions of pieces called "Bunte Blätter," "Jugend-album,"
&c., were made up of short sketches written for the
most part in the early period of his career, but not
included in any of the former sets of pieces. Among
the duets, the Andante and Variations for two
pianofortes (op. 46) is pre-eminent. The work was
at first written for two pianofortes, two violoncellos,
and two horns, and it is curious to find in one or two
of the variations traces of the composer's original
intention. In the eighth variation, for instance, the
leading phrase has evidently been transferred from
the horn part.

Compared with the other piano works, the delightful
duets called " Bilder aus Osten " are very late in order
of composition, coming as they do after the opera
" Genoveva."

Before leaving this branch of our subject, we must
warn the student of Schumann's pianoforte works
against placing any reliance in the metronome marks,
which are quite incorrect in all the existing editions, the
composer's own metronome being altogether out of
order. Madame Schumann, in the edition of her
husband's pianoforte works which she is at present
preparing for the use of students, intends to indicate
the correct time of the compositions by new metronome
marks.

Concerning Schumann's own pianoforte playing,
those who heard him most frequently tell us that he
produced an extraordinary richness of effect and depth

of tone ; that his accentuation was very slight, and that he used both pedals with the greatest freedom, sometimes, it would seem, at the expense of clearness. His predilection in favour of the frequent use of the pedal appears throughout his works ; a certain peculiarity in his method of directing its use is to be noticed ; he employs no sign, as all other composers do, for the momentary lifting of the pedal at a change of harmony, but reserves the asterisk commonly used at such points for passages where the pedal is to be dispensed with altogether, leaving to the discretion of the player the management of its necessary and constant intermission. An amusing story, *apropos* of Schumann's playing, is told in Jansen's " Davidsbündler." The composer used often, in the dead of night, to sit at his piano and play by the hour together, giving the reins to his imagination. An industrious, but too practical, piano-player, who lodged in the same house with him, struck with the romance of the situation, determined to follow his example ; accordingly one night when the moon was flooding the room with light, and all things contributed to a romantic effect, this sentimental person rose from his bed and betook himself with passionate emotion to his instrument, and played—the first of Cramer's studies !

CHAPTER V.

SONGS—CONCERTED AND ORCHESTRAL WORKS.

THE year 1840 was an eventful one in Schumann's
life, and affected his artistic development as much as it
did his outward circumstances.   The crisis of his love-
story had come : the long years of suspense were over ;
the object of his true and enduring affection was won ;
and henceforth the current of his life was changed.
The fanciful romance of the " Davidsbund," which had
given rise to so many beautiful creations, was forgotten,
and replaced by interests and emotions of a more actual
and substantial kind.   Instead of a morbid habit of
introspection, we now find in him a keen insight into
human character; and instead of self-analysis, sympathy.
The very form of composition to which he devoted
himself exclusively during this momentous year—the
song—led him to seek inspiration outside himself, since
the choice of subject, and to some extent the limitations
of form, lay not with himself, but with another.   With
the same whole-hearted devotion that he had previously
brought to bear on pianoforte writing, he now applied
himself to the art of setting words to music.   We found,
in reviewing the pianoforte works, that none of the
best in that class were written subsequently to 1839,

and a similar phenomenon meets us here : nothing but songs were composed in the year of Schumann's marriage, and none of the greatest and most famous songs date from any other year. There are indeed many fine songs contained in the larger vocal works, which are of later date ; but these are for the most part of a dramatic order, and we are speaking of the song proper, that is to say, of a lyrical entity, indepen-dent and self-contained. There is one respect in which the comparison with the pianoforte works does not hold good ; in those we can trace the composer's gradual progress from a condition of immaturity to one of absolute perfection, but in the songs no such advance is to be perceived. Not that all the songs attain to one level of excellence, but their difference in value depends on quite other conditions than those which limited him in the pianoforte works. They vary, not any longer in the point of structure, but in the amount of imaginative power and truth of delineation which they display. In some of the songs we feel that the common expression " set to music " is the only true one ; there is no indis-soluble bond of union between words and music, nor is there any reason why later composers should hesitate to write music to the same words. But in others, and these are by far the most numerous class, the marriage of " perfect music unto noble words " has indeed been brought about ; the poem seems to have waited incom-plete until the creation of the music which itself inspired, and any other setting of the words, though it may have many points of value, seems little short of sacrilegious.

This power of putting himself on a par with the poet

whose words he sets, and entering completely into his mind, is the quality that distinguishes Schumann from the earlier song-writers. In the songs of Beethoven, however fine the words, they appear as nought in comparison of the music, and the same may generally be said of Schubert, though in certain isolated instances, especially where the words are by Goethe or Heine, the composer has succeeded in attaining to the perfect balance between words and music, so that neither is subordinate to the other. Who, for instance, can read the " Erlkönig " without thinking of Schubert's setting ? But it is possible to read "Ich denke dein," or even " Kennst du das Land," without the thought of any one of the many songs which these words have suggested.

But what was the exception with the older composers becomes the rule with Schumann. Not in a song here and there, but throughout entire cycles of songs, he follows his poet's varying moods, amplifying and idealizing his thoughts, but never assuming more than a just equality. Of all the songs, the set called " Dichterliebe," written to sixteen of the short poems which make up the " Buch der Lieder " of Heine, are the most characteristic in this respect. In considering these songs, we cannot divide Schumann's work from Heine's, or think of the two men separately ; each bears an equal share in the effect produced, and indeed it is sometimes impossible to rid ourselves of the impression that the songs are the work of one man, not of two. Not one of all those subtle touches of pathos, humour, or passion, which make Heine's poetry what it is, is lost upon Schumann ; so absolute is the assimilation,

and so well is it sustained, that it is next to impossible
to say which are the best and truest of the songs,
though in point of technical vocal treatment they are
not so equal. Schumann's songs are in many moods,
but there is not one of these that is unrepresented in
the "Dichterliebe;" this must be our excuse for going
more into detail with this set than with any other. The
idyllic grace of Nos. 1—3, 5, 8, 12, and 15, is re-echoed
again and again, as for instance in "Wenn ich früh in
den Garten geh'," "Aufträge," or "Dein Angesicht."
Nos. 4, 10, 13, and 14, with their calm openings and
their infinitely sad endings, such as none but Heine
could have written, and none but Schumann could have
set, find parallels here and there among the other
settings of words by the same poet; and even "Ich
grolle nicht," which has never been even approached
in its isolation of passionate despair, has more than one
companion in point of sustained emotion, as "Wid-
mung" and "Stille Thränen." No. 9, in which the
voice has only the subordinate part to play, connects
itself with "Es leuchtet meine Liebe," a conception
of rare beauty, but one which cannot be appreciated or
realized as a song; it is only when it is heard in another
shape, as the Scherzo of the string Quartet in A minor,
that the full meaning and poetry of the idea is brought
out. In No. 6, the music reflects not only the meaning
of the poem, but also the impression made upon
Schumann by the solemn grandeur of Cologne.

That power which he had exercised since the first days
of his musical life, of expressing in music the personal
characteristics of his friends, was now and henceforth
directed into a new channel. No longer do we meet

with those portraits of individuals, real or imaginary,
which are of such constant occurrence in the pianoforte
works; instead of these, he reproduces for us, as here,
the impression that certain places, especially towns,
have made upon his imagination.   One instance occurs
in the pianoforte works : the " Faschingsschwank aus
Wien " gives, as we have said before, the most vivid
picture of Vienna, as it affected the composer.   In
another song, " Stirb, Lieb, und Freud," we seem to
breathe the very air of Augsburg, or of one of the
storied cities of Germany.   A nobler example than any
we have mentioned is a passage in the " Rhenish "
Symphony, where Cologne is again the subject.   Of
this we shall presently speak more in detail.   No. 11
is in some ways the most wonderful of the set; in its
mixture of humour and tragedy, the music is as
thoroughly in the spirit of Heine as are the words.
To this song there are two parallels, "Abends am
Strand," and " Der arme Peter," both set to Heine's
words, and both giving musical expression to that
mirth of Heine's which seems always on the verge of
tears.   It has been well said, " What Schubert was to
Goethe, Schumann was to Heine."   The last of the set,
No. 16, may claim to rank with the ballads, which are
no less remarkable in their own way than the lyrical
songs.   A merely narrative poem like Chamisso's
" Löwenbraut " might well fail to kindle Schumann's
imagination; in this class, too, it was for Heine to
inspire his best work, by the poem of " The two Grena-
diers," in which the composer saw an opportunity for
bringing in his favourite " Marseillaise."   The manner
in which the idea of the soldier's death is conveyed in

the closing chords of the accompaniment, is most striking, and may serve as another instance of the sympathy between the author and the composer.

Hardly less wonderful, though in an entirely different way, is the Lorelei ballad called " Waldesgespräch," which occurs in a set of songs written to words by Eichendorff, and called " Liederkreis." This song, with its feeling of weird and irresistible fascination, is intensely powerful in effect, and is conceived in the truest spirit of romance. Others of this set, as " In der Fremde," No. 1, " Mondnacht," and " Frühlings-nacht," are of exquisite beauty, but as a whole they are not equal to the " Dichterliebe," nor have they that continuity and connection which is so remarkable an element in another cycle of songs, the " Frauenliebe und Leben." The words, by Chamisso, are not of a very high order ; but the music to which they are set reveals to us an extraordinary depth of penetration into a side of human character which men are generally supposed incapable of understanding—the intensity and endurance of a pure woman's love. Few of the songs are widely known, except, perhaps, " Er, der herrlichste von allen ;" all are at least interesting, but the master-touch appears quite at the end, in the short instrumental *coda* which summarizes all that has gone before, and welds all the songs into a perfect whole, just as is done in the " Dichterliebe."

The songs of Schumann are often charged with being unvocal; this is in a measure true, inasmuch as it requires a cultivated and sympathetic musician, rather than a mere vocalist, to sing them with proper effect ; but when this condition is fulfilled, there are no songs that can compare with these for passionate intensity and depth of emotion.

In 1841, the year immediately succeeding the " song-year," the composer's chief though not exclusive attention was turned to orchestral composition, three out of the five symphonic works having been written at this time. Since, however, an examination of these productions would lead us into a later period of Schumann's career than the one we are now engaged upon, it will be better to defer it till we have considered the concerted or chamber compositions, to which the next year was wholly devoted.

As in 1840, nothing but songs was written, and all the best date from that year, so in 1842 nothing but chamber music was written, and Schumann's master-pieces in this branch of art saw the light at this time. The first production was that which we know as op. 41, consisting of three Quartets for strings alone. Considered without reference to the instruments for which they are written, these show a perfection of form which can only be accounted for when we remember the attention he had given in the previous year to symphonic structure; but viewed as string Quartets, they are by no means perfect. The composer has not succeeded in freeing himself from the influence of the pianoforte, nor has he as yet attained to the power of investing the stringed instruments with that combination of independence and interdependence which characterizes all the masterpieces in this kind. The first of the three, in A minor, is undoubtedly the best; it suffers less than the others from the defects we have just mentioned, and its intrinsic beauty and individuality have procured for it a certain degree of celebrity, though this is as nothing when compared to the fame of the two great compositions of this year, concerning which we shall speak immediately. The other two Quartets stand in F and A major; the latter is the more remarkable, since it contains many passages in which may be perceived the germs of similar subjects in the Quintet.

The Quintet in E flat (op. 44), for pianoforte and strings, has earned for itself a position second only to the finest works of Beethoven. Here in England, it has outlived the howls of execration with which it was at first greeted by the sapient critics, and at the present time no more generally popular piece of concerted music can be found, unless it be the "Kreutzer" Sonata of Beethoven. And it is not only admired and beloved by cultivated musicians—among these no dissentient voice will be found—but it can also be enjoyed, though of course in a more limited degree, by the general public, and even by the lowest class, socially speaking, that can be got together, as has been proved over and over again, when it has been played to audiences in the East end of London, and listened to with the greatest and most evident pleasure. The perfection of its form and structure; the variety and spontaneity of its lovely melodies; the breadth of its technical treatment in all the parts; the magnificent effects of sound; the unceasing contrasts now between the movements themselves, now between their several subjects, as for instance in the Scherzo and its two Trios, or in the solemn march and its central section, or even between the pianoforte and the strings; all these qualities combine to make the Quintet the masterpiece of Schumann's work in this sphere of composition, and to raise it to a point at least as high as any piece of chamber music that the world has seen since Beethoven.

The Quartet for pianoforte and strings, also in E flat (op. 47), is second only to the Quintet among Schumann's works. It is not at first easy to see why it has not attained to as great a degree of popularity as its companion, for it is no less spontaneous and original : the first movement is as vigorous, and the last as bright, as the corresponding portions of the Quintett; and the " romantic " element is quite as strong in the gloomy Scherzo and in the passionate Andante, with its bitter-sweet suspensions, as it is in the middle movements of the earlier work. The Scherzo of the Quartet, like that of the Quintet, has two Trios, and of these the second bears a curious resemblance, and one for which there is no accounting, to a passage near the end of the first movement of the " Faschingsschwank." The sombre colouring of this movement may perhaps partly account for the difference in popularity between these two works, the greatest of Schumann's chamber compositions ; but another reason may be found in the fact that whereas a perfect balance subsists between a quartet of strings on the one hand, and the pianoforte on the other, a trio of stringed instruments cannot so easily be used as a contrast to the piano alone.

The only other work of 1842 is one which serves to show that the composer intended to have enriched the list for this year with a pianoforte Trio. The " Fantasiestücke " for piano, violin, and violoncello (op. 88), are infinitely below the level attained in the other

F

productions of the year : they were no doubt meant at
first for a Trio, but were considered to lack the continuity which this title would require, and so were called
by the humbler name they now bear.

For five years Schumann desisted from chamber
compositions, and it was not till 1847 that the first
works which deserve the name of pianoforte trios were
written. The first, in D minor (op. 63), is full of passion,
and bears traces here and there of that gloomy restless-
ness which gradually overshadows the production of
this and subsequent years. This character is apparent
only in the first and third sections; the Scherzo and
the Finale are delightfully fresh and healthy in their
tone. The second Trio, in F major (op. 80), is far
brighter and more generally attractive than the first;
while more graceful, it is however less impassioned,
except indeed in the Adagio, which is one of the most
deeply felt utterances of its composer. The third Trio
dates from 1851, and was written between the two
violin Sonatas, which we shall shortly have to consider.
Its key is G minor, and its opus-number 110. In no
respect can it compare with the other Trios, for the
gloom of the author's later years has settled upon it so
as not merely to give colour to the subjects on which
the music is built, but even to render the form obscure.
A curious return is made in the Finale to the mood of a
work written in very different times, the Fantasia in
C (op. 17), with the central movement of which the last
section of the G minor Trio has much in common.

Finer by far than this work are the violin Sonatas
which precede and follow it in the list for 1851. They
are in A minor and D minor, and are numbered opp.

105 and 121.   The first is the more generally known of
the two, but both contain many passages of great
beauty and individuality.   Schumann's favourite device
of alluding to a former movement in a later one, is
used in the slow movement of the second Sonata with
the happiest possible effect.   There are a good many
sets of separate pieces for the piano and one other
instrument ; of these the most important are the three
Fantasiestücke for piano and clarionet, op. 73, and the
well-known set for piano and violoncello called "Stücke
im Volkston," op. 102.   A set of three Romances for
oboe and piano, op. 94, also deserves mention ; though
not familiar to the public in their original form, they
have become more or less widely known through the
medium of an arrangement of the oboe part for the violin.

Between the concerted chamber music and the orchestral works stands a class of composition which was
in its ordinary use foreign to Schumann's nature, and
in which he has only left us one example of surpassing
merit.   The essential idea of the Concerto, at least in
the modern acceptation of that term, involves the
thought of display ; in all the classical models of the
form, constant opportunities are given for the soloist
to show off his powers to the best advantage, and in
most examples a blank space is left which the performer
is expected to turn to account as best he may.   Now it
is not needful to have studied Schumann's character
very deeply to know that nothing could be more
thoroughly antagonistic to all his artistic convictions
than such personal display as is here implied.   Yet he
could not fastidiously reject a form that all the great
masters had used with success, and that had been found

so effective in the hands of his great contemporary, Mendelssohn. Thus it came about, that in 1841, when he was engaged upon orchestral composition, he wrote an Allegro for pianoforte and orchestra, completing it in 1845 by the addition of the other movements which unite with it to form the great pianoforte Concerto in A minor, op. 54. The Allegro is not in strict form, excepting that the piano has a solo marked Cadenza near the end, a section, by the way, that seems to belie the essential purpose of a Cadenza, inasmuch as it starts, not faster than the rest of the movement, but at exactly half the pace, with the utmost deliberation. The solo part has plenty of difficulties, and many of its passages are extremely brilliant, but it is not allowed to usurp attention for long together; the orchestral treatment is throughout so interesting, and the combinations of effect are so skilfully managed that the hearer is compelled to listen more to the composition as a whole than to the solo part as the most prominent feature of attraction, and so the idea of personal display is successfully kept in the background. The charm of the musical dialogue in the Intermezzo, and of the cross-rhythm in the second subject of the Finale, has never been surpassed in any work of the master's, and as a whole the Concerto must be allowed a very high place among his compositions. Two other works for piano and orchestra exist, numbered 92 and 134 respectively; they are both in the same form, an Allegro with an introduction. Though they contain many interesting passages and points of beauty, they cannot hold their own beside the Concerto of which we have just spoken.

A Concerto for violoncello and orchestra, op. 129, and a similar work for four horns and orchestra, op. 86, are more remarkable for their extraordinary technical difficulty than for any great amount of intrinsic musical beauty, except in the slow movement of the violoncello composition.   One work for violin and orchestra, a Fantasia dedicated to Joachim, is printed as op. 131, and another, a Concerto in four movements, remains still unpublished.   Besides this Concerto the same great artist possesses a musical curiosity of very great interest in the shape of a Sonata for violin and pianoforte, written conjointly by Albert Dietrich, Johannes Brahms, and Robert Schumann, on the occasion of Joachim's visit to Düsseldorf in 1853.   Schumann's part in the affair consists of a beautiful Romance and a somewhat lengthy Finale.

The orchestral works of Schumann have not yet attained, in England at least, to anything like the degree of popularity which has been universally accorded to his pianoforte and chamber compositions, as well as to the songs.   It is not very easy to account for this.   Dating as most of them do from the finest period of the composer's career, and the happiest of his life, they are full, as we might expect, of beauties of the most exquisite kind, and in some respects they are surpassed by none of the other works.   In all the Symphonies, and in all their parts, the greatest possible freedom and nobility of invention is displayed; the treatment of the subjects is unconstrained, ingenious, and thoroughly original; and there are many points in the orchestration which astonish and delight us, even in the earliest examples, by their newness and beauty of effect. It is not till we come to examine his ordinary treatment of the orchestra that we are able in any degree to explain the fact that the Symphonies are less widely known than almost any class of Schumann's compositions. In listening to these Symphonies, or indeed to any of the orchestral works, one can hardly resist a certain feeling of heaviness and oppression, not by any means in the subjects themselves, or in their treatment, but in the way they are set before the hearer. The constant doubling of the string parts by the wind, and of one half of the wind band by the other, produces an effect of thickness in the sound which detracts to no slight extent from the beauty of the subjects, especially at their first appearance, when clearness is above all to be desired. We can well understand that to an audience accustomed to the fairy lightness of Mendelssohn's orchestration, Schumann's must have seemed terribly wanting in brilliancy; but with the broader views of art which are now gaining ground among us, we may be sure that these Symphonies will increase year by year in popularity, until they are accepted at their true value.

Of an early attempt at orchestral composition, made in the year 1832, we have already made brief mention. Beyond the fact of its being in G minor, little is known concerning it; it was given in public and in its entirety on a certain memorable occasion in Zwickau, when the composer first saw and heard Clara Wieck. The work which is always reckoned as the first Symphony is in B flat major, and numbered op. 38. It was written, like two of the other symphonic works, in 1841, the year in which he began to turn his attention in good

earnest to orchestral writing. When we remember
the great happiness that had just crowned his hitherto
unsatisfied life, we need not wonder at the genial
freshness and placid beauty that breathes from every
page of the score. The meaning of the whole becomes
clearer to us when we know that Schumann originally
meant to call it " Spring Symphony." The first movement was to have represented " Spring's awakening,"
and the last " Spring's farewell." To those purists
who, forgetful of Beethoven's Ninth Symphony, object
to the introduction of a triangle into the score of a
Symphony, this explanation of the first intention of the
composer may not be unacceptable; they will perhaps
allow the obnoxious instrument to remain, on condition
of its carrying with it some spring-like suggestion.
The rest of the world, meanwhile, will contentedly
admire the effect produced, without seeking out any
specially vernal phenomenon as an excuse for an inno-
vation upon stereotyped form.

In connection with the opening bars of the Symphony a circumstance is related by Dr. Spitta, which
shows the inexperience of the composer in rather
a characteristic way. The introductory phrase was
originally identical with the first eight notes of the
chief subject of the Allegro; on the B flat horn,
however, the notes G and A are "stopped" notes,
while the B flat is naturally produced, so that a
most ludicrous effect resulted at the first rehearsal,
and one which amused Schumann as much as it did
any one else. The difficulty was overcome by trans-
posing the whole phrase a third higher. Side by side
with this proof of the composer's deficiency in tech-

nical knowledge, it is extraordinary to find instances of the greatest boldness of orchestral treatment. Thus the slow movement is no more remarkable for its intrinsic beauty than for the newness of its effects. Among these the most prominent is the passage for the trombones at the end, by which the way is prepared for the Scherzo. There are two Trios to this, as to so many others of Schumann's Scherzos; in the charming dialogue of the first we catch a faint reminiscence of a passage in the first movement of the "Faschingsschwank." Another reminiscence of a pianoforte work, namely, the last of the "Kreisleriana," occurs as an episode in the last movement, which, if it were only more lightly orchestrated, would yield to none of its composer's works in point of attractiveness.

The second work of the year is one from which its author with characteristic modesty withheld the title of Symphony only because it lacked a slow movement. Thus the composition in E major (op. 52), has been always named "Overture, Scherzo, and Finale;" of the first movement Dr. Spitta has observed that it "offers us the only example to be found in Schumann of the influence of Cherubini, a master for whom he had a great reverence." The Scherzo is highly original, and its Trio, both in itself and in the way it is introduced, is perfectly contrasted with it. The Finale, which underwent considerable alteration in 1845, is not of very great interest; indeed the work as a whole must be admitted to be decidedly inferior to the Symphonies properly so called.

Second among these last, in order of composition, stands the Symphony in D minor (op. 120), which, like

the two works we have just noticed, was written in
1841, two months after the Overture, Scherzo, and
Finale, but subjected to a complete revision in 1851.
In its later form it appeared after the other Symphonies,
and has therefore been generally called the fourth of
the set. The alterations in the score were confined
for the most part to a redisposition of the wind band,
and to the omission of a guitar, which was at first
included in the accompaniment of the Romanza, its
place being taken in the new recension by the *pizzi-
cato* strings. In regard to musical form, this work
has one feature of absolute novelty, which is notified
in the sub-title "Introduction, Allegro, Romanze,
Scherzo, und Finale in einem Satze" (in one movement). Not only is no pause made between the four
sections of the work—there was a precedent for this
in Mendelssohn's "Scotch" Symphony—but there is
an essential unity and interconnection between what
would in ordinary circumstances be called the movements, which is entirely original. In an autograph
copy in the possession of Joachim, yet another title is
found: "Symphonic Fantasia," which implies that the
composer desired more freedom of form than could be
found within the limitations of the ordinary Symphony.
It is a favourite device of Schumann's to allude in one
movement to a passage or subject which has occurred
in a former one, but nowhere is this artifice employed
so constantly or with so good an effect as in the D
minor Symphony. A certain arpeggio-like figure which
appears at first in the introduction in the most un-
obtrusive way conceivable, turns out to be nothing
less than the motto of the whole work. It is the chief

subject of the ensuing Allegro, and it is there used with a pertinacity, and varied with an ingenuity, in the highest degree remarkable. Thirty-five bars after the commencement of the second half of the Allegro, it appears in conjunction with an episode which is ultimately to become the chief subject of the Finale, though even there it will be accompanied by the same motto-phrase. During the Romance and Scherzo the motto is unheard, but it reasserts itself in a passage of surpassing grandeur, which is used to lead into the finale. The Romance is exquisitely tender and is orchestrated most effectively. Of the phrase taken from the Introduction we have already spoken ; from this is developed an episode surrounded by lovely figurations on the solo violin. This episode is shortly afterwards heard as the trio of the passionate Scherzo, and it is used again with great effect to prepare the way for the wonderful interlude before the Finale. The last movement affords, in its second subject, one of the very few instances in which Schumann can be accused of having adopted the idea of any other composer. The similarity, nay, identity, between this and an episode in the Larghetto of Beethoven's second Symphony, has been often pointed out, and indeed it could hardly escape the observation of any person acquainted with both works. Of all the Symphonies, if that in B flat is the brightest and happiest, that in D minor is by far the most passionate and deeply felt.

We now have to consider a work dating from 1846, just halfway between the first and second recensions of the D minor Symphony. Written, or at least sketched, as Schumann himself tells us, at a time of

great physical suffering, the Symphony in C major
(op. 61) is to be regarded as reflecting the struggle of
the composer's spirit with the overpowering depression
induced by his bodily weakness. "The first movement," he says, "is full of this contest, and its character is one of caprice and defiance" (*launenhaft,
widerspenstig*). The motto of this Symphony—for
like its companion in D minor it has a motto—is the
trumpet-call with which it opens; it is used less constantly, but is more striking when it appears, than the
arpeggio in that work. It reappears at the close of
the Scherzo, and forms an important factor in the
coda of the Finale. The Scherzo is no less defiantly
capricious than the first movement; it is in 2—4 time,
and has two Trios, the first of which is one of those
charming dialogues between wind and strings that
are so characteristic of Schumann, while the second is
an example of wonderful ingenuity and beauty of orchestral effect. It is impossible to convey in words
any idea of the beauty of the slow movement. In
addition to its felicity of invention, its passionate
expression, its clearness of form, and originality of
instrumentation, it has a feeling of perfect maturity
and repose which raises it to a higher level than either
of the former slow movements. Its subject is brought
in again with the happiest results in the working out
of the Finale, which forms a vigorous close to this most
interesting work. One peculiarity of form which it
has in common with the Finale of the D minor Symphony may be mentioned. After the "working-out"
the first subject does not reappear, but in its stead a
new subject is introduced. This subject, in the C

major Symphony, though new as regards that work, is
not new in music, for it has done duty before in one
of Beethoven's songs, " An die ferne Geliebte," and
also in the Andante of Mendelssohn's " Hymn of
Praise." It is so perfectly fitted for its present position, however, that it is only the most captious of
critics who would find fault with it for not being entirely new.

Between this and the next Symphony there is again
an interval, this time of four years. The last of the
Symphonies, in E flat (op. 97), is almost the last work
of its author of which it may be said that no falling-off
in power, no decrease in brightness, and no signs of
the final morbid condition of his mind, can be perceived.
In 1850 he had just taken up his abode at Düsseldorf,
and, as we have seen, he looked forward to his new life
there with the brightest hopes. The " Rhenish " Symphony, as it is generally called, reflects this sanguine
mood with the utmost clearness ; nor is that all, for it
portrays most distinctly the impression produced on
the composer by the new scenes in which he found
himself. He tells us himself that it was the first sight
of Cologne Cathedral that suggested the composition
to his mind. During a visit to that city Schumann
was present at Archbishop von Geissel's elevation to
the cardinalate, and the effect produced on his imagination by the ceremony found expression in the fourth
movement of the Symphony, to which he at first
intended to give the title " In the style of an accompaniment to a solemn ceremony " (im Charakter der
Begleitung einer feierlichen Ceremonie). He discarded
this name, however, before the publication of the work,

as he had the " Spring " names in the B flat Symphony,
explaining his objection to such titles in the words,
" One must not show his heart to people ; a general
impression of a work of art suits them better; then
they at least draw no wrong comparisons." The
whole work is instinct with the poetry and romance
which are to the German mind inseparable from the
Rhine and its neighbourhood ; it is thoroughly national,
and it need not surprise us to find it much more
popular in style, and more generally appreciated than
the other Symphonies. The Scherzo, with its Volks-
lied-like subject, is the most charming, as the fourth
is the most solemn movement to be found in the
Symphonies; the latter, which serves to prepare the
hearer for the bright Finale, is a marvel of constructive
ingenuity and orchestral effect.

Concerning the Overtures, the only other works
written by Schumann for orchestra alone, we need not
go into any degree of detail ; nor can we do better
than quote Dr. Spitta's excellent summary of them in
his article on Schumann in Grove's Dictionary :—

" The poetical Concert-Overture, invented by Mendelssohn, and practised by Bennett and Gade, was a
form never cultivated by Schumann. His Overtures
are ' opening pieces,' whether to opera, play, or some
festivity or other. In this again he follows Beethoven.
His Overtures, like those of Beethoven, are most effective in the concert-room, when the drama or occasion
for which they were composed is kept in mind. It is
so even with the wonderful ' Genoveva ' Overture,
which contains something of Weber's power and swing;
but more than all it is true of the Overture to Byron's

' Manfred,' so full of tremendous passion. None of the Overtures subsequently written by Schumann reached this degree of perfection, least of all his 'Faust' Overture, though that to the 'Braut von Messina' (op. 100) is not much inferior to 'Manfred.' In the last year of his productive activity Schumann was much occupied with this form, but the exhausted condition of his creative powers cannot be disguised, either in the 'Faust' Overture or in those to Shakespeare's 'Julius Cæsar' (op. 128), and to Goethe's 'Hermann und Dorothea' (op. 136), which last he had intended to set as an opera. The festival Overture on the 'Rheinweinlied' (op. 123) is cleverly worked, and a very effective *pièce d'occasion.*"

CHAPTER VI.

CHORAL, NARRATIVE, AND DRAMATIC WORKS.

THE compositions to which the above title is to be applied date, one and all, from the period of Schumann's life which we called the third, viz., the years 1843—1856 ; indeed, the first work of the kind, " Paradise and the Peri," was written in the first year of that period. Of the composer's friend, Emil Flechsig, who now appeared as the translator of Moore's words, mention has been already made. Much alteration was necessary before the poem could be effectively set to music, and this alteration was undertaken by Schumann himself. The resulting libretto was fitted to music which in construction approaches more nearly the oratorio than any other form, since the dramatic element is modified, if not removed, by the employment of a " narrator." This feature has in some quarters been objected to on the ground that it is imitated from the Passion-music of Bach ; but the objection is a purely superficial one, for Schumann uses not merely one particular solo voice, but different soloists, and even chorus, to deliver the narrative portions of the text. Though Moore's poem contains much that is eminently suited to musical treatment, there is yet a certain similarity in the incidents and in the way they are told, which makes it difficult, if not impossible, to avoid some degree at least of monotony. So much being admitted, as it will be by those who have given any attention to the subject of the musical capabilities of words, it cannot be denied that Schumann's first attempt to set a long narrative poem to music is wonderfully successful. It is not until the third part, which treats of the Peri's ultimate success, that the interest begins to flag, or any feeling of monotony to be experienced. The first scene or part is exceedingly fine; the interest of the music is well sustained, and a climax of very great beauty is obtained in the Finale, "For blood must holy be." In the chorus which describes the Indian conqueror, nothing can be more admirable or more thoroughly characteristic of the composer than the reticence and moderation which led him to abstain from employing in the accompaniment any of those bizarre effects of orchestration which another musician might have delighted in, and used with no sparing hand. Noble as is the close of the first part, it is far eclipsed by more than one section of the second; the Chorus of Genii and the Quartet, "For there's a magic in each tear," are beautiful in different ways; the scene between the dying lovers, and the final dirge, are intensely pathetic, and show the dramatic side of Schumann's art, a side that is more rarely revealed than any other. Part III., even when the episodes which hamper its action are omitted, cannot but strike the hearer as unnecessarily long, though the opening chorus is as graceful, and the ensemble, " O blessed tears," is as impressive as anything in the work. If the whole could have concluded

with the number last mentioned, the feeling of anti-
climax, which is now produced by the Finale, would
have been avoided. Notwithstanding the drawbacks
we have pointed out, the beauties of the work are
sufficiently numerous and striking to admit it to a very
high place among Schumann's compositions, and to
warrant us in endorsing the composer's conviction,
expressed in a letter, " A soft voice seemed to say
while I wrote, It is not in vain that thou art writing."

The list of Schumann's works for the years 1846—
1849 contains a large number of choral compositions,
for the most part short in extent, and comparatively
unimportant. It will be remembered that during that
time the composer held the post of conductor of a
choral society in Dresden, a post vacated by Hiller on
his removal to Düsseldorf. The choruses we have
mentioned were doubtless written for this society, and
we need not be surprised to find them suffering from
that want of spontaneity and inspiration which is the
besetting sin of nearly all such *pièces d'occasion.* The
best are the "Jagdlieder" (op. 137), for male chorus,
with an *ad libitum* accompaniment for four horns, and
the Motett, "Verzweifle nicht" (op. 93), for double
male chorus. Among the choral works of 1849 there
are two to which the remark just made does not apply.
The "Requiem for Mignon" (op. 98) is one of the most
delicate and sympathetic works that ever came from
Schumann's pen. It would be impossible to imagine
any setting of the exquisite passage in "Wilhelm
Meister" which would reflect more faithfully the spirit
of Goethe's purest conception. The other exception is
the setting of Hebbel's "Nachtlied" (op. 108), which

G

displays greater power of choral treatment than any earlier work for chorus alone. Beside the choral works of this period there are three compositions for concerted solo voices which may be spoken of in this connection, since they date from the same year as the "Requiem" and the "Nachtlied." The "Spanisches Liederspiel" (op. 74), the "Minnespiel" (op. 101), and the "Spanische Liebeslieder" (op. 138), are all in the same form, that, namely, of a song-cycle in which the separate members are now allotted to a single voice and now set as Duets or Quartets. The arrangement has a wonderfully good effect, and the cycles are among the most attractive works of the composer, though they have not hitherto attained the popularity to which they are entitled. Of late years, however, the form has found such wide acceptance through the medium of the beautiful "Liebeslieder" of Brahms, that we may hope that Schumann's cycles, which doubtless suggested the form to the younger composer, may soon reach at least an equal measure of renown.

Of the circumstances which led to the composition of Schumann's single opera, we have spoken in another place. The reader will remember that he was obliged to construct his own libretto, having been unable to induce Hebbel to modify his sensational play of "Genoveva" to suit his (Schumann's) ideas of what an opera should be. His praiseworthy efforts to soften down the horrors of the drama and to bring it more into harmony with Tieck's dramatic poem on the same subject, unfortunately resulted only in the diminution of the power and interest of the play. The character of Golo, the servant to whose care Genoveva is confided by her too trusting husband, and who betrays his trust in the most infamous manner, first assailing the lady's virtue, and then, in revenge for her resistance, traducing her to his master, is one for which the sympathies of an audience cannot possibly be enlisted.   The expedient of making him act in obedience to the commands of the witch Margaretha, and thus transferring some of the responsibility of his guilt to her, is not very success-ful, nor does it tend to strengthen his character.   Nor when we come to consider the music are matters much better in this respect.   Golo's lovely song in the first act is false to his character as it is revealed in the later scenes.   If his sin had been one which proceeded from uncontrollable passion moved by a sudden impulse, if we had been permitted to see him repentant, not merely remorseful, and if he were represented as confessing his crime to the master whom he had outraged, then the first song might be regarded as true to his better self.   But the pertinacity with which he urges his hateful suit, and the diabolical ingenuity of the plan by which his revenge is brought about, preclude the charitable supposition suggested at the opening.   A suggestion was made to Schumann by a well-known musical *savant* in Leipzig to the effect that a scene between Golo and Siegfried should be inserted near the close of the opera, to satisfy poetical justice.   But even the contemplation of such a scene was too painful for the tender-hearted composer, and so the opera lost a number which would have given it that dramatic intensity and propriety which it now lacks.   Another passage which, though of great beauty so far as music is concerned, is yet terribly undramatic, is the opening scene of Act III. In fact the only part which has consistency and truth is that allotted to the long-suffering heroine, whose character is, more than any other, capable of lyrical treatment. But once consider the work from a musical point of view alone, and it will be found full of beauties of the highest order. The whole of the first act, and more particularly the march and the tenor solo,—the first Duet and the Finale in Act II.,—the opening of Act III., and many passages in the magic-mirror scene, where Margaretha shows Siegfried the fictitious evidences of his wife's guilt,—Genoveva's solo and the ensemble before the Finale of the last act,—all these are but examples of the musical beauty which goes through the whole. Like Weber's " Euryanthe," from which, by the way, Schumann got several suggestions, " Genoveva " must live by its musical beauty alone; and the fact that it has hitherto had but a precarious hold upon the operatic stage of Germany is a matter for regret rather than surprise.

Though " Genoveva " is the only opera, properly speaking, composed by Schumann, there is another work intended for theatrical performance, which, small as it is in extent, is entitled to a very high position among the master's works. The music to Byron's " Manfred " (op. 115) was written, like the greater part of " Genoveva," in 1848. Though dramatic in form, the poem is so essentially undramatic in character that its presentment upon any other stage than that of Germany is out of the question. There, however, it is still occasionally performed, in conjunction with Schumann's music. The work has few, if any, of the elements which make incidental stage music effective.

Like "Genoveva," it must be judged exclusively as pure music, without reference to its theatrical purpose, and as a poetical transcript in music of the feelings excited in the reader of Byron's drama. The overture, a serious and impassioned composition, which would seem to have been written first, without reference to the rest of the music, is perhaps the best of Schumann's overtures in point of sustained power and interest. Of the vocal portions, the choruses are the best, showing as they do a greater freedom and ease of treatment than any former choral work of the composer's; the Hymn of the Spirits of Ahrimanes, and the final Requiem, are particularly fine. The invocations in the earlier scenes are less interesting; the absence of dramatic treatment makes itself unpleasantly felt. The finest sections are the "melodramas," all of which have great musical beauty, though their dramatic connection with the passages they are intended to accompany is of the slightest. The whole scene between Manfred and Astarte suggested an orchestral number of the greatest refinement and sympathetic beauty. A characteristic instance of the composer's gentleness of disposition as contrasted with the gloom of the poet whose words he was illustrating, is found at the close of the "Manfred" music, where the Requiem Chorus sheds over the final moments of the drama a glow of hope that is not even suggested in Byron's work. It has been truly said that the music, in spite of its great beauty, finds its proper place neither on the stage nor in the concert-room; its effects are too delicate and subtle, and not sufficiently dramatic for the theatre, and on the other hand it is difficult to keep the action of the play before the minds of a concert audience. If the "symphonic poem" had been invented in Schumann's day, or rather, if it had at that time acquired the general acceptance it has since obtained, the " Manfred " music would have been a perfect example of the form, for as a poetic rendering in music of the impression produced by the play, nothing can be finer or more deeply felt than Schumann's composition.

In musical importance, as in extent, the " Scenes from Goethe's Faust " are to be regarded as the greatest work of his later years. It is, moreover, of the highest interest to the student of the composer's life, for in no other of his productions are we allowed, as we are here, to trace the gradual decadence of the artist's powers from their fullest and most mature vigour to their final condition of obscurity and gloom. The composition of the scenes occupied no small part of his attention during a very considerable period of his life, for the first scene in order of production was completely sketched out in 1844, and the Overture, which was written last of all, dates from 1853, the last year of his creative activity. In 1848 the great division of the work which stands as Part III. was completed by the composition of the Chorus, " A noble ray." It is occupied solely with the last scene of the second part of the play, the Epilogue in heaven, which treats of the final salvation of Faust. It was this noble scene which first inspired Schumann to undertake the task of setting to music passages from the most important poem of modern times. The mystical leanings of his earlier days awoke again to find their true fulfilment in the pure and spiritual ecstasy of Goethe's vision.

Taken alone and as a complete entity, the "third part" may be considered as Schumann's masterpiece. All his noblest qualities as a composer are here seen to the best advantage; his purity of emotion, his keenness of spiritual insight, here find their proper sphere, in a work the like of which no other composer has ever attempted. The highest degree of celestial exaltation, which others have now and then reached at supreme moments of briefest duration, is by Schumann sustained throughout the seven scenes which make up the last division of the work. Even the short intro-ductory chorus, with its expression of heavenly calm, raises the hearer into a region far above the earth. The solos of the three anchorites, the music of which is an admirable example of the composer's use of contrast, and the graceful Chorus of happy spirits of boys, lead most effectively into the scene of Faust's salvation, beginning "A noble ray of spirit-life." This number, composed, as we have said, no less than four years after the rest of Part III., is surpassed by none in variety and wealth of imagination. The effect of the little Quartet, "We with all joy receive him" is unspeakably beautiful; it is no doubt partly due to the strange tonality, and to its extreme simplicity as compared with the rest of the number. The fine scene which follows, and in which Doctor Marianus, Gretchen, the penitents and the Mater Gloriosa appear, is again the work of 1844; it prepares us in the best possible way for the splendid final scene, the "Chorus mysticus," which is one of the most beautiful of Schumann's creations, and certainly the most elaborate vocal composition ever written by him, being set for eight part chorus and solo voices, and treated in the richest polyphonic style. After the Chorus had been written some time, the composer considered that its latter part, from the opening of the Allegro in F major, " The ever-womanly beckons us on," had too much the air of earthly enjoyment, and that it did not, with all its intricacy of construction, reach the level of spiritual purity which he had set himself to attain. He therefore rewrote the Chorus from that point to the end, and in many ways the work of 1847, for from that year the second recension dates, is to be preferred to the original version ; it is more ethereal in character, its construction is not so visibly elaborate, and there is no alloy of earth in its happiness.

Between the completion of the third part, and the composition of those scenes which followed it in chronological order, only one year elapsed, but that was the most prolific year of Schumann's life, 1849, in which no fewer than thirty works, each bearing a separate opus-number, were written; the mere interval of time therefore hardly represents the real space between the sections, or accounts for their difference of style. The work of 1849 consists of Part I. and the first half of Part II., ending with the sunrise and Faust's awakening. The opening scene, in the garden, is tender and idyllic, but without any special power or charm; its effect is greatly impaired by the orchestration, which the composer intended to make full and massive, but which he only succeeded in making heavy. In this and the fol-

lowing number, Gretchen's prayer, a certain lack of
form is perceptible, which entirely deprives them of
the interest with which they would, no doubt, have
been invested had they been written in Schumann's
earlier years.   The scene in the cathedral, which begins
with a dialogue of no great interest between Gretchen
and the evil spirit, ends with the solemn strains of the
" Dies iræ," but there is a lack of impressiveness about
the scene which it is extremely difficult to account for.
Wasielewski says very truly, "To paint the terrors of
the Last Judgment was not given to him; he had
another artistic mission to fulfil."   The "Ariel" scene
at the beginning of Part. II., set for soli and chorus,
is the finest section outside the third part; it is exquisitely graceful, as befits the subject, and its elaborate
construction helps rather than hinders the effect.
After the sunrise, a scene set for tenor solo, the accompaniment to which is orchestrated with much of the
composer's old power, the awakened Faust (baritone)
has a long song of considerable length, with which the
portion written in 1849 closes.

The next year saw the completion of the scenes
which close the second part and treat of the death
of Faust.   The sombre character of these scenes fell
in with the composer's mood, and the music is
full of power which may fitly be called graphic,
though not dramatic.   The work was now finished
all but the Overture, to the composition of which
Schumann looked forward with something like ap-
prehension.   To compose an Overture to " Faust,"
understanding by that name not one but both parts
of Goethe's poem; to give, within the narrow limits

of the form, any foreshadowing of the innumerable
elements in the drama; and to provide a fitting introduction to musical scenes, many of which had been
written years before—this was a task before which
the boldest of composers might well have quailed.
At the beginning of 1851 he expressed himself thus (we
quote from Wasielewski) : " I am often haunted by the
thought of having to write an Overture to the 'Faust'
scenes, but I am convinced that this task, which I
regard as the hardest of all, can scarcely be satisfac-
torily achieved; the elements that have to be mastered
are too many and too gigantic.　But yet it is necessary
that I should preface the music to 'Faust' with an instrumental introduction, for otherwise the whole will
not be rounded off nor the various moods fitly ushered
in.　Yet it cannot be undertaken on the spot; I must
await the moment of inspiration, then it will get on
quickly.　I have been much occupied, as I have said,
with the idea of a 'Faust' Overture, but as yet nothing
has come of it."　The moment of inspiration did not
arrive till 1853, when the powers of the composer were
all but exhausted.　All things considered, the failure
of the Overture in point of artistic merit was a foregone
conclusion.　A work of art which is so far from being
spontaneous that its author dreads to undertake it,
could scarcely succeed, even if the other conditions
were as favourable as possible; taking into considera-
tion, therefore, the existing circumstances in this case,
we shall not be surprised to find the " Faust " Overture
what it is, an obscure and gloomy composition, which
has the air of having been left without those finishing
touches which would in earlier years have been applied

to it, and would have given it the necessary clear-ness.

In the last years of the composer's public life, he returned to a form that he had used with success in one instance, " Paradise and the Peri." The form of the short ballad set for soli, chorus, and orchestra, com-mended itself to the wearied imagination of Schumann as presenting ideas of a picturesque and romantic kind in a small compass.   Five works in this form are among the latest productions of the master.   In 1851 were written, " Der Rose Pilgerfahrt" (op. 112) and " Der Königssohn " (op. 116) ; in 1852, " Des Sängers Fluch" (op. 139) and " Vom Pagen und der Königstochter " (op. 140) ; and in 1853, " Das Glück von Edenhall " (op. 143).   Of these the first, the accompaniment to which was first written for the piano alone, the orches-tral setting being an afterthought, is by far the best, since it contains one or two numbers, notably a dirge, in which the musical treatment is well sustained, and something of the old power displayed.   Many beautiful ideas are, as we might expect, to be found here and there in the other ballads, but on the whole they are by no means satisfactory.   The narrative portions are executed in a perfunctory style, as though the parts that took Schumann's fancy had been written first and the connecting links added afterwards, when his interest in the subject had begun to fade.   Besides these, Schumann wrote in the last year of his creative activity two ballads for declamation, but they have little claim upon our notice beyond their novelty in form.

Among Schumann's works, there are very few com-positions to which the word " sacred " in its ordinary sense can be applied. That this arises from no want of sympathy with, or reverence for, the highest purpose and object of art, appears most clearly in a letter written in January, 1851, in which the following passage occurs: "To apply his powers to sacred music must ever remain the loftiest aim of the artist. But in youth we are all too firmly rooted to earth with its joys and sorrows; with advancing age the branches stretch higher. And so I hope that the time for my efforts in this direction is not far distant." In a former chapter mention has been made of his intention of undertaking an Oratorio; the scheme fell through, but the idea bore fruit in the shape of a Mass and Requiem, both written in 1852, and numbered op. 147 and op. 148 respectively. Both seem to have been intended rather for sacred concerts than for the church service, and the arrangement of the former is at variance with the ritual of the Catholic Church. Its best numbers are the "Credo" and "Sanctus," in the latter of which the orchestration and arrangement are especially fine. The Requiem contains many interesting passages, but that which is generally the most effective section of the service, the hymn "Dies iræ," is the weakest portion of the music. He would almost seem to have been hampered by the very familiarity of the words, and to have been unable to give them satisfactory musical expression. Far better are the settings of two hymns by Rückert for Advent and the new year, (opp. 71 and 144 respectively), both set for soli, chorus, and orchestra, and both showing strength of construction, and the highest earnestness of purpose. Not only did the words offer a new field to the composer

but since the hymns date from 1848 and the beginning
of 1850, it is not surprising to find in them more
sustained power than is to be seen in the later works
of which we have just spoken. In considering the
choral, and more especially the "sacred" works of
Schumann, we are irresistibly driven to the conclusion
that to this most sympathetic of composers, from
whom the knowledge of no emotion in the individual
heart was withheld, it was a matter of extreme difficulty
to give expression to collective emotion, or to those
feelings which affect the whole of mankind in common.
That power, granted to Mendelssohn in so remarkable
a degree, was denied to Schumann. Those who would
see what Schumann can do in the realm of sacred
music must go to the third part of "Faust," to the
Requiem for "Mignon," or the close of the "Manfred"
music, all of which are on behalf of individual per-
sonages, though they are sung by a chorus. A short
song of exquisite beauty and purely devotional character, also entitled "Requiem," and set to words attri-
buted to Heloisa, the beloved of Abelard, must not be
forgotten in this connection; it is contained in the
collection published as op. 90.

At the close of our survey of the composer's works,
a passing mention must be made of one of the last
efforts of his expiring genius. Just before the clouds
that were to obscure his intellect, and ultimately his
life, gathered thick around him never to disperse, he
made a return to that form of composition in which he
had in early years created so many enduring masterpieces. The set of "Five Morning Songs" ("Gesänge
der Früh," op. 133) for pianoforte solo, must ever be

intensely interesting to the lover of Schumann's character as well as of his music. In spite of many
beautiful passages there is much that is gloomy, and
the forms, except in the case of the first piece, lack
conciseness; still now and then we come upon ideas
and phrases that have something of the brightness
suggested in the title. Connecting themselves as they
do by their form with the earliest efforts of the composer, they serve to bind together the whole circle
of his works, works which, whatever their musical
merit in relation to the productions of other composers, have certainly never been surpassed in respect
of the various kinds of interest that attach to their
composition.

CHAPTER VII.

SCHUMANN THE CRITIC.

It will be remembered that for a period of almost exactly ten years the composer devoted himself with great assiduity to the interests of a musical paper of which he was one of the original founders, and ultimately the editor—the *Neue Zeitschrift für Musik*. Authorship was no unaccustomed pursuit to Schumann, for in very early days we hear of his helping his father in some of his literary work, and no doubt he would be thoroughly familiar with the business of publishing. When we consider his early training, to say nothing of his years of university study, we need not be astonished to find him possessed of such literary power as has been exhibited by no other practical musician before or since, with the single exception of Richard Wagner. But even more remarkable than his literary talent is his power of discerning the merits and demerits of musical compositions, in other words, his critical faculty. It has often been asserted, and it is to a certain extent true, that the creative faculty cannot coexist with the critical, and that an artist can no more judge of the works of other artists than he can of his own. Schumann stands as a lasting refutation of this assertion, or perhaps as the most prominent exception to the rule. He possesses the critical faculty to an extent that has never been equalled, at all events in connection with music. There is no quality to be desired in a musical critic which Schumann does not possess. That his artistic aims and tenets were of the purest and highest, will not be questioned even by the most superficial observer of his life and works. The object of his own critical labours, as of the journal which is inseparably connected with his name, was "the elevation of German taste and intellect by German art, whether by pointing to the great models of old time, or by encouraging younger talents." To this maxim Schumann adhered through life. Unlike most critics, he found, or seemed to find, praise easier than blame. In the great mass of criticisms, from the first article in praise of Chopin contributed to the *Allgemeine Musikalische Zeitung* in 1831, to the final eulogy of Johannes Brahms, dated 1853, expressions of grave censure are few and far between. Whatever is praiseworthy receives its meed of praise; faults are extenuated wherever it is possible, and in the case of the errors of youth the composer is corrected in the kindest way imaginable, and encouraged to do better. In reading, after the lapse of so many years, his opinions of men who have since become well known,—opinions pronounced for the most part upon some very early work,—it is wonderful to see how in nearly every case the verdict of later years has confirmed his judgment.

Scattered up and down his "Gesammelte Schriften," there is, besides the criticisms of composers and their works, an abundance of sentences concerning music in general which are worthy of a place among the established and unalterable rules of art. "A true master draws to his feet not scholars, but masters." "The artist is to choose for his companions those who can do something besides playing passably on one or two instruments,—those who are whole men, and can understand Shakespeare and Jean Paul." "'It has pleased,' or 'It has not pleased,' say the people. As if there were nothing higher than pleasing the people." "To send light into the depth of the human heart—that is the artist's calling." Concerning the critical faculty : "I speak with a certain diffidence of works of whose precursors I know nothing. I like to know something of the composer's school, of his youthful aspirations, his examples, and even of his actions and the circumstances of his life,—in a word, of the man and the artist, and what he has done hitherto." "A musical work is to be regarded from four points of view,—from that of form (the whole, the separate divisions, the periods, and the phrases), of the musical composition (harmony, melody, construction, elaboration, style), of the particular idea intended to be represented, and of the spirit that inspired form, material, and idea." Speaking of the difficulty of judging a work before hearing it performed, he says : "Though the inner hearing is the finer musical organization, yet the spirit of the performance has to be considered, and the bright, living sound has its peculiar effects, concerning which even the good musician, who can, as it were, hear through the eye from the paper, may be deceived." Besides the well-known " Rules for young Musicians," which need

H

not be quoted here, we find many hints of the greatest
value on the subject of early musical training. In
reviewing the performance of an infant prodigy, which
he does with exceeding kindness, these remarks occur :
" Manual dexterity should be developed as quickly as
possible into virtuosity. But that feat whereby our
young musicians have mostly obtained that name we
must withstand as utterly false—that, namely, of extempore playing in early life." " Do not put Beethoven
too soon into the hands of the young; steep and
strengthen them in the fresh animation of Mozart."

More important than the general aphorisms about
music are the opinions upon particular musicians, and
of these the most interesting to the reader of our own
day are the criticisms upon composers who were already
famous when Schumann wrote, or who have since
become so. The names of many composers of the
generation that is now passing away would not at this
day be so well known as they are, but for some friendly
word in the *Neue Zeitschrift*, without which their merit
would never have become known. As we have said in
an earlier chapter, there was no paper existing at the
time when the *Neue Zeitschrift* was started in which
young composers could hope for anything like a fair
criticism of their works. The importance of Schumann's work, therefore, on the musical history of the
present century, can hardly be over-estimated. It
may not be uninteresting to gather from his writings
passages in which his opinion of the great composers
of different times is expressed.

His admiration of Bach is unbounded. Among the
most beautiful of the author's prose compositions is

one in which he describes how he tried to find the grave of the great master, and received from the sexton the answer to his inquiry, "But there are so many Bachs;" after which he turns to the description of Mendelssohn's playing of one of Bach's organ chorales, with the reflection that fame is something different from a tombstone. The "Crucifixus" in the Mass in B minor is called "a piece that is only to be compared with other things of Bach, one before which all masters of all times must bow in reverence." In another place he calls him "the greatest composer in the world."

Concerning Handel we find very little except a casual remark on his popularity in England.

Of Dom. Scarlatti he says : "The marshalled array, so to speak, of Bach's ideas is not to be found in him ; he is far more superficial, fugitive, and rhapsodical; it is difficult always to follow him, so quickly are his threads interwoven and loosed again ; in relation to his time his style is short, pleasing, and piquant."

A movement by Couperin "has a Provençal touch and tender melody."

Of Mozart's "Figaro :" "The music to the first act I consider the most heavenly that Mozart ever wrote."

The most important utterance concerning Beethoven is contained in the four articles, signed Florestan, Jonathan, Eusebius, and Raro respectively, upon the subject of a monument to Beethoven. Elsewhere he says of the C minor Symphony : "Often as it is heard, both in public and in private, it exerts unaltered power in every age of life, like many great natural phenomena, which, often though they are repeated, yet fill us ever afresh with fear and wonder."

The chief tribute to the memory of Schubert is the splendid history and analysis of the Symphony in C major, which, it will be remembered, was brought to light by means of Schumann, and in which he naturally felt a special interest. The article, which was written with the pen that Schumann found lying on Beethoven's grave, is delightful from beginning to end, and abounds in short graphic touches, some of which, like that in which he describes the Symphony as "heavenly length" (*himmlische Länge*), will only be forgotten when the music itself shall have passed into oblivion.

In a review of one of Cherubini's Masses the following admirable touch occurs: "Those passages which sound even secular, out of place, and almost theatrical, belong, like the incense, to the Catholic ceremonial, and affect the imagination so that one seems to have before one's eyes all the pomp of that service."

For Weber he has all the romanticist's sympathy. "Euryanthe" is spoken of in terms of unqualified admiration, which is not surprising when we remember what an influence that work had on "Genoveva." "The opera cost him a piece of his life. True; but through it he is immortal." It is "a chain of brilliant jewels from beginning to end."

For another eminent romanticist, our own John Field, he has "nothing to say but unending praise;" and for Field's greater disciple, Chopin, he cherished the most affectionate admiration throughout his life. On his behalf that extraordinary first-fruit of Schumann's literary undertaking, "Ein Werk II.," of which mention has already been made, was written. Those who know and love Chopin's later works may not thin⸗

the " La ci darem " variations in any respect remarkable ; all the more then must they wonder at Schumann's discernment of the promise which they contain.
In a review of his second Concerto, Schumann, in the
character of Eusebius, says : " He had his education
from the greatest,—from Beethoven, Schubert, and
Field.   We may suppose him to have received from
the first his daring spirit, from the second his tender
heart, and from the third his facile hand."   One of
the best and wisest articles in the collection is one in
which some of Chopin's pianoforte works are reviewed,
and in which the composer is warned against confining
himself to pianoforte writing, since there is a danger
of his reaching no higher a level than that which he
had already attained.   The article is doubly interesting as it is dated 1841, and thus was written just
after Schumann had emancipated himself from his exclusive devotion to piano composition.   The final sentence is very characteristic : " The Waltz " (op. 42, in
A flat, with the cross-rhythm) " is, like his earlier ones,
a drawing-room piece of the noblest kind ; if he were
to play it at a ball, thinks Florestan, at least half the
ladies who danced ought to be countesses."   Chopin's
admirers will hardly agree with Schumann's opinion
of the Funeral March, and the movement which follows
it ; in a review of the whole Sonata, this passage occurs :
" There follows, even gloomier, a Marcia Funebre,
which has something almost repulsive in it; in its
stead an Adagio, perhaps in D flat, would have had
an incomparably more beautiful effect.   Then what
comes in the last movement under the heading
' Finale ' is more like a mockery than music.   Yet

one must admit that even from this unmelodious,
joyless movement a peculiarly weird spirit holds us
in its thrall, so that we listen till the end, spell-
bound, powerless to resist its influence, without
murmur,—but also without praise ; for music it is not.
So closes the Sonata as enigmatically as it began, like
a sphinx in mocking laughter." For the gloomy side
of Chopin's nature Schumann had little sympathy.
A notice of the Tarantelle (op. 43), couched in no
favourable terms, is followed by a review of Sterndale
Bennett's Rondo Piacerole (op. 25), which begins with
these words : "After the composition just mentioned
Bennett's seems like a dance of the Graces after a
witches' revel."

For the composer last named Schumann had a
warm affection, both as a man and as an artist. From
the time of his arrival in the musical world of Leipzig,
the "Gesammelte Schriften" are full of the most appreciative notices of his works. Appreciative they
are in the truest sense, for while their author shows
that he has no slight predilection for Bennett's style,
he yet is able to estimate him at his true value, fully
recognizing the fact that he cannot claim a place among
the greatest composers, though he deserves a very high
one among those of less exalted rank. He is earnestly
recommended to devote himself to orchestral compo
sition, and to attempt the larger forms of art. He is
"to turn from what is elegant and playful, and to find
a language for strength and passion."

The figure that is most prominent in Schumann's
writings, and that may be considered the hero of the
"Gesammelte Schriften," is that of his greatest con

temporary, Mendelssohn. Each work of the composer's, as it is published or performed, is greeted
with the most generous and enthusiastic acclamation.
A passage, which is as remarkable for justice as for
beauty, must be quoted from a review of "St. Paul."
He calls it "a work of the purest kind, a work
of peace and love. It would be wrong, and would
displease the poet, to compare it with the Oratorios
of Bach or Handel. In so far as all church compositions, all sacred buildings, or all pictured Madonnas
have something in common, they are alike; but Bach
and Handel wrote when they were men, and Mendelssohn wrote almost as a youth."

He speaks of the Trio in D minor as "the master-
trio of the present time, just as, in their own time,
were the Trios of Beethoven in B flat and D, and
that of Schubert in E flat." In the same article we
meet with one of Schumann's most pregnant utterances; he calls Mendelssohn "the Mozart of the 19th
century, the man who mostly clearly discerns and
reconciles the contradictions of our time." He then
proceeds: "And he will not be the last composer.
After Mozart came a Beethoven; the new Mozart
will be succeeded by a new Beethoven, ay, he is
perhaps already born." In all Schumann's writings,
nothing is more remarkable than his absolute freedom
from jealousy, which in his position in relation to
Mendelssohn might have been so easily stirred up
in a less generous nature. At different times during
their lives attempts were made to bring the two
greatest musicians of their time into opposition, but
as far as Schumann was concerned, he was guiltless

of even an envious thought. In this connection a
good anecdote is given in Jansen's "Davidsbündler,"
to the effect that a certain celebrated musician spoke
slightingly of Mendelssohn in Schumann's presence.
The latter sat silent for a time, as his custom was,
but at length he got up, took the speaker by the
shoulders, and with the words, "Sir, who are you,
that you dare to speak thus of a master like
Mendelssohn?" left the room.

Among the men of lesser achievement, Heller and
Henselt receive almost unqualified commendation, and
their names are among those of most frequent
occurrence. The value of the former is well summed
up in the following sentence: "He possesses an extraordinary power of arranging the mediocrities of
other composers, so that they sound like good original
compositions. We hardly know any other composer
who resembles him in being able to lose so little of
his dignity in a form which, from an artistic point
of view, must always be looked upon with a certain
suspicion. Let him bestow some of his wealth upon
the amateur; for him he will build a bridge that
will lead to the understanding of the deeper mysteries
of art. He need not fear that his own better powers
will thereby be impaired."

Vieuxtemps, who in another branch of art is akin
to these last, is called "the most gifted of our younger
masters, who already stands so high that one cannot
contemplate his future without a secret dread."

A considerable space is devoted to Berlioz, the
latest and most extreme of the Romanticists. His
Symphony called "Épisode de la vie d'un artiste"

is minutely analyzed in one of the longest and most detailed of Schumann's reviews. Great admiration is expressed for his new orchestral effects, as for his boldness and originality, while at the same time the critic is by no means blind to his defects, as for instance the poverty of his melodies and the lack of sustained power. In the course of an interesting review of the " Waverley " Overture, he says, " Berlioz's music must bè heard to be appreciated," and " One does not know whether to call him a genius or a musical adventurer." Apropos of the meanings which had been looked for in this Overture, he makes this characteristic protest : " Heavens, when will the time come when we shall no longer be asked what we mean by our divine compositions; look for the fifths and leave us in peace." Several other articles on Berlioz not contained in the " Gesammelte Schriften " are given by Jansen. In one of these we meet with an utterance of Schumann's in later life : " I expressed my opinion that there was a divine spark in this musician, and hoped that riper age would purify and glorify it to the clearest flame. Whether this wish has been fulfilled I know not, for I am not acquainted with the works of Berlioz's mature manhood."

Liszt comes in for more commendation than we should have expected Schumann to bestow. Speaking of his great set of studies, he says : " His own life stands in his music. Taken early from his fatherland, thrown into the exciting atmosphere of a large town, wondered at even as a child and as a boy, he appears in his earlier compositions now as longing for his

German home, and now as frivolous, and brimming with the light froth of the French nature."

It is deeply interesting to find him criticizing the performances and productions of her who, as Jansen says, "filled his life with the sunshine of love." When Clara Wieck was a mere child, her playing drew from Schumann his second prose composition, an article contributed in August, 1832, to a periodical called the *Comet*, and couched in terms of the most enthusiastic admiration. In the following year he says, in writing to a friend concerning her, "Think of perfection, and I will agree to it." In the last letter of his that has been published, which bears the date of January, 1854, he alludes to his wife's rendering of his latest work, the "Morning Songs," in a manner which shows that his opinion of her supreme artistic powers had undergone no change. In the *Neue Zeitschrift* her figure, generally veiled under one of the Davidsbündler disguises, is of frequent occurrence, and some of her compositions are reviewed. It is not difficult here and there to discern the lover beneath the critic's mask, although in no instance can the author be accused of undue partiality.

Among the younger men whom Schumann helped to usher into fame, Gade receives the greatest amount of attention, his early works being exhaustively and most wisely criticized. The critic evidently delights in the musical possibilities in the composer's name, noticing that the letters which compose it are identical with the names of the open notes on the violin. On the occasion of Gade's departure from Leipzig, Schumann wrote in his album a little musical setting of the words " Auf Wiedersehn " (*au revoir*), using as a bass the notes *G a d e* and *a d e* (farewell).

Among the later articles there is one dated 1848 in which a set of songs by Robert Franz is sympathetically reviewed, and the composer hailed as a transmitter of the true traditions of the song-form. The criticism is all the more valuable as coming from one who, three years before, had written some of the most beautiful songs that have ever been given to the world.

By far the most significant of the articles which have for their object the encouragement and vindication of young musicians is that entitled, " Neue Bahnen," of which mention has been already made. Written in 1853, long after the author had given up his literary work altogether, it brings before us the figure of the composer, at the end of his course, consciously and formally handing on the high traditions of classical form to a rising, youthful genius whom he feels to be worthy of them. And that Johannes Brahms has kept them pure and undefiled will not be doubted or denied by any musician by whom his works have been carefully and thoroughly studied.

The *Neue Zeitschrift* was exceedingly successful, and naturally had considerable influence in the world of music. Many a composer with such an influence at command, would not have scrupled to use it on behalf of his own productions, nor would much blame attach to such a procedure. But to the high-minded nature of Schumann nothing could be more abhorrent. The casual reader of the " Gesammelte Schriften ' would scarcely suspect, if he did not know beforehand, that the writer was a composer at all, for the infrequent allusions to his own works are so cursory when they do occur that they might well escape observation. The longest criticism of a work of his own occurs in an article on Franz Liszt, that artist having played the " Carnaval " at one of his own concerts. After devoting considerable attention to the other numbers in the programme, he gives a very short account of the origin and general scope of his composition,— in which, by the way, he alludes to the lady to whom the " Carnaval " was dedicated as " a musical acquaintance,"—and goes on to say : " Though there is much that may please one person or another, yet the moods of the music are too constantly changing for an entire public, that does not want to be scared off every minute from one thing to another, to follow." In letters to intimate friends he speaks, on rare occasions, more freely about his productions. One of the most interesting letters given by Jansen is addressed to Verhulst, and bears the date June, 1843. It contains the following passage: " Much in my Quintet and Quartet will appeal to you ; there is in them real life and movement. The Variations for two pianofortes, &c." (see p. 61), " I have just heard for the first time ; they did not go particularly well. They will have to be practised ; their mood is very elegiac, and I think I must have been rather melancholy when I wrote them."

In the case of two composers, Schumann has often been accused of forming and pronouncing an unfair judgment, or at all events one in which the majority of cultivated musicians cannot agree. These two are

Meyerbeer and Wagner. His opinion of the former was certainly in the highest degree unfavourable. In his criticism of the "Huguenots" he makes the nearest approach to invective that is to be found in his writings. Before we join in the accusation, we must remember that Schumann's artistic convictions were diametrically opposed to the operatic method and style of Meyerbeer, who never hesitated to sacrifice whatsoever did not add to the stage effect, or to use means which must be admitted to be meretricious in order to gain his ends. The delicate details by which Schumann attained, in his songs, his wonderfully true delineations of character and emotion, were altogether out of Meyerbeer's reach; but on the other hand they are utterly unsuited to the theatre, where they produce very much the same effect as if the subtlest touches of Turner's hand had been applied to scene-painting. Another thing which will be perceived by the careful reader of the article in question, and which will help to exonerate the author from the charge brought against him, is that he attacks, not so much Meyerbeer himself, as those foolish admirers of his who wished to claim for him a place in the highest rank of composers. Could Schumann have foreseen the present position of Meyerbeer in the estimation of musicians, and have realized that no one would wish to place him beside Mozart, Beethoven, or even Mendelssohn, he would surely have hesitated to pour out the vials of his wrath. Perhaps his bitterest expression, if expression it can be called, occurs in the "Theaterbüchlein," a group of short operatic criticisms given at the end of the collected writings, where the heading

"Prophet von Giac. Meyerbeer" is followed by nothing but the date and a little black cross, as though to indicate a wish that the dead composition might rest in peace.

The passages in the "Gesammelte Schriften" in which Wagner's name occurs are certainly, on the whole, of a disparaging kind. But only one of the short paragraphs in which he is mentioned refers to him as a composer. Of the others, one finds fault with his additions to Gluck's "Iphigenia," and one with his reading and interpretation of "Fidelio." Schumann had quite enough of the purist in his disposition to prevent his approving of any innovations in the score of a classical work, but be this as it may, nothing is said of Wagner as a writer of stage music, except in the few lines that refer to "Tannhäuser," in which Schumann forbears to criticize the work in detail, withholding his ultimate opinion till a later occasion. He fully recognizes the claims of the opera to a more thorough examination, while confining himself to the following remarks, which are all the criticism he gives his readers : "It certainly has a stroke of genius. If his music were only as melodious as it is spirited, he would be the man of the time." This criticism is not to be taken as the author's final opinion, for he afterwards wrote a longer and more appreciative notice of the same work, which, however, does not appear in his collected writings. We cannot look for very enthusiastic admiration of Wagner from Schumann, for what was said above concerning Meyerbeer holds good, though in a far less degree, of Wagner, who, though he never sacrifices anything

to stage effect, yet uses it as an important factor in
his work. There was thus a divergence in artistic
tenets between these two great men, and it was not
lessened in their personal relations. Their opinions
of each other are placed in amusing juxtaposition in
E. Hanslick's "Musikalische Stationen." Wagner expressed himself thus to the author in 1846 : " Schumann
is a highly gifted musician, but an *impossible* man.
When I came from Paris I went to see Schumann ; I
related to him my Parisian experiences, spoke of the
state of music in France, then of that in Germany,
spoke of literature and politics, but he remained as
good as dumb for nearly an hour. Now one cannot
go on talking quite alone. An impossible man ! "
Schumann's account, apparently of the same interview,
is as follows : " I have seldom met him, but he is a
man of education and spirit; he talks, however, un-
ceasingly, and that one cannot endure for very long
together."

If after all the critic is to be accused of narrowness
of view in the case of these two composers, there are
numberless passages in the collected writings which
prove that, as a rule, his opinions were broad enough
to please the most eclectic and universal of music-
lovers. Though in one place he says of Rossini, " He
is the most excellent scene-painter,—but take away
from him the artificial light and the seductive distance
of the theatre, and see what remains," he reckons the
" Barbiere " as one of the " first comic operas of the
world," the others being " Figaro," and Boieldieu's
" Jean de Paris," and in another place he speaks of it
as " cheering, spirited music, the best that Rossini has

ever written." No work of Bellini's is directly
criticized, but his name is not unfrequently mentioned,
and sometimes almost with approbation.   There is a
characteristic story in Jansen's book, which tells how
he suspected himself of having been moved to ears by
an aria of Donizetti's, and how he was greatly relieved
when he succeeded in proving to his own satisfaction
that it was the voice of the singer, not the beauty
of the music, that had touched his heart.

In the earlier part of the collection we find a rich
fund of humour perpetually revealing itself, as well
as a vein of gentle satire which is used more often to
soften the sting of the blame that is to be bestowed
than to give it an additional poignancy.   A Sonata by
a certain count who was addicted to amateur composition is reviewed by " Eusebius," who affects to treat
it as the work of a young lady, and to give the
imaginary composer much good advice couched in the
most courteous terms.   At the close " Florestan "
adds the words, " How slily my Eusebius goes round
about !   Why not say plainly, the count has much
talent, but has not studied enough."   In a review of
twelve studies by Cramer he feigns that the title-page
has been lost, and makes various guesses at the composer's name, according to the style and character of
each study.   In writing of some young lady's *rondo*,
he lessens the severity of his criticism by couching it
in English.   After a punning allusion to her lack of
heart, and her similarity in style to *Herz*, he goes on :
" The hand yields not in whiteness to the keys it
touches. I could indeed wish that the Diamonds which
adorn it existed in the mind,—yet I would take the

hand, if You would give it me, with this single promise
on your part, that You would never compose anything."
Speaking of the four Overtures to "Fidelio," he
thanks the Viennese of 1805 for their want of appreciation of the first Overture, in consequence of which
the world was enriched by the other three. A very
prolific composer is told that "if he had not got to
his op. 250 he would be farther on," implying that his
desire for publicity has hindered his artistic progress.
The scholastic Philistines are well described : " According to them Beethoven never wrote a fugue, nor was
he capable of writing one, and even Bach allowed
himself liberties over which one can but shrug one's
shoulders; the best instruction is only to be got from
Marpurg."

He had a pleasant way of reviewing a mass of music
that was not very interesting. He makes the music
appear as a subordinate accessory in a narrative or
sketch. In an article called " The Psychometer " he
describes with much elaboration a purely imaginary
machine, which is supposed to answer questions concerning the merits of musical compositions inserted in
it. Schumann's opinion of the works to be reviewed
is of course given as an example of the use of the
instrument. In an article dated 1835, and quoted by
Jansen, the criticism of some pianoforte pieces is inter-
spersed with scraps of overheard conversation, real or
imaginary. An article called " Tanzliteratur " notices,
among other things, compositions by Schubert and
Clara Wieck, and gives a most poetical account of
the lady's playing, calling her "Zilia" throughout.
Another batch of dance music, among which are

waltzes by Chopin and Liszt, is reviewed under the guise of a description of a ball, where of course the works to be criticized form the programme. It is throughout most amusing, and one passage which describes a certain Ambrosia hammering out a waltz by Liszt with great and visible effort, is not unworthy of Jean Paul.

Occasionally Schumann ventured into the region of pure fiction, without reference to his critical function. A fable of considerable length, written with a polemic intention, in answer to some virulent attacks that had been made upon him and his paper, will be found in Jansen's book, where also the circumstances which led to its composition are given in full. Perhaps the most touching and sympathetic of all Schumann's prose writings is an article, or rather a sketch, called "The Old Captain," the central figure of which is evidently drawn from the life. Besides many pathetic and humorous touches, it contains a beautiful description of the ideal relations between performer and listener. "To no one could I play better, or with greater pleasure, than to him. His listening elevated me; I swayed him and led him whither I would, and yet it seemed to me that it all came first from him."

One of Schumann's most characteristic traits, both as a critic and as a man, was his kindness to young musicians just on the threshold of their career. Of the many instances of encouragement shown in the course of criticism, one will suffice to quote. A young singer had failed to produce any effect on the audience in consequence of extreme nervousness. Schumann wrote: "Nervousness is known to make itself felt most in the higher notes, and once or twice the singer missed her entry, a thing which has happened to a thousand singers before her." A delightfully interesting account of a visit paid to Schumann in 1840 is given by the pianist Amalie Reiffel, and quoted entire by Jansen; she describes her own feelings at being obliged to play to the composer, and his kind reception and treatment of her, in a most graphic and charming manner. To another, and a far greater artist, he spoke words of kindly encouragement, which have been retained with affectionate remembrance ever since. When Joseph Joachim first visited Leipzig as a boy of thirteen, he played one evening at Mendelssohn's house. After playing the "Kreutzer" Sonata with his host he happened to sit near Schumann, who, having remained silent for some time, at last leant forward and pointed to the stars, which were shining into the room ; then, patting Joachim's knee, he said, "Do you think they know up there that a little boy has been playing down here with Mendelssohn ? "

CHAPTER VIII.

SCHUMANN AND HIS CRITICS.

THE reader of the lives of Mendelssohn and Schumann
cannot fail to be struck by the contrast between the
two careers. To the one, public life must have seemed
one long triumphal procession. From the time of his
arrival at Leipzig, when he was received with open
arms by the entire musical world, until his early death,
the enthusiastic adulation of the public never for an
instant waned. On crowds and on individuals alike,
the magical fascination of his personality exerted an
influence that was irresistible. When from Mendelssohn's pen were pouring in ceaseless rapidity compositions that could be understood and loved at once by all
who heard them, it was little wonder that the public
had no time or inclination to give to the work of Schumann that attentive study by which alone they can be
properly appreciated. Not that he was intentionally
ignored; the public at large could scarcely be expected
to realize his musical merits for themselves, and besides
this, he was almost entirely unknown in society, chiefly
owing to his silent, reserved manner and disposition.
We in England, who are accustomed to look upon
Madame Schumann with an additional interest and
reverence on account of her alliance with the composer,

can scarcely realize that at one time his chief claim to notice, in the eyes of the German public, lay in the fact of his being her husband. Yet such was the case, as there is abundant evidence to show. It is related that after she had played at one of the small German courts, her serene host asked her with great affability, " If her husband was also musical ? "

Though he was so completely unknown to the general public, there were yet a select few, critics and others, by whom his works were appreciated and keenly admired. In the first letter of Schumann's appended to Wasielewski's " Life," an account is given to the writer's friend Töpken of an appreciative criticism which had just appeared in the *Wiener Musikalische Zeitung* (No. 26, 1832), and which the composer goes to the trouble of transcribing. The article, which refers to the " Abegg " Variations and the " Papillons," was written by the poet Grillparzer; considering the time at which it was written it is remarkably appreciative, and even reminds us now and then of Schumann's first criticism of Chopin, though it is inferior to that article both in musical knowledge and in imagination. The young composer's boldness and independence are fully recognized: " He belongs to no school, but creates of himself without making any parade of outlandish ideas, collected together in the sweat of his brow; he has made himself a new ideal world in which he moves almost as he wills, and with a certain original *bizarrerie*."

Another favourable critic of some of Schumann's early works was Franz Liszt, who wrote in the *Gazette Musicale* for Nov. 12th, 1837, a thoroughly sympa-

thetic and intelligent criticism of the Impromptus, op.
5, and the two Sonatas, opp. 11 and 14. In giving
his opinion of the composer's works as a whole, he says
with great truth, "The more closely we examine
Schumann's ideas, the more power and life do we discover in them; and the more we study them, the more
are we amazed at the wealth and fertility which had
before escaped us."

From the great French romanticist, Hector Berlioz,
there came no direct criticism of any work of Schumann's, but from an expression in one of his letters we
gather that he entertained at least a high respect for
his powers. He says that the Offertorium from his
(Berlioz's) "Messe des Morts" met with unexpected
success, and "won the invaluable approval of one of
the most remarkable composers and critics of Germany,
Robert Schumann."

The two Sonatas which Liszt had reviewed in the
Gazette Musicale were sent to Moscheles for notice in
Schumann's own paper. Beside the criticism itself,
which would naturally be of the most favourable kind,
there are some words quoted in Moscheles' "Life," from
his diary, which show that the writer only expressed
his true sentiments in the published article.

He says (we quote from Mr. A. D. Coleridge's trans-
lation), "For mind (Geist), give me Schumann. The
romanticism in his works is a thing so completely
new, his genius so great, that to weigh correctly the
peculiar qualities and weakness of this new school
I must go deeper and deeper into the study of his
works."

One of the most prominent figures in the musical

world of Schumann's time was Moritz Hauptmann, the cantor of the Thomasschule in Leipzig, and the most eminent theoretical musician of his day. In the highly interesting series of his letters to Hauser, Schumann's name occurs very rarely. In one place, speaking of the pianoforte works in the year 1839, he calls them "pretty and curious little things, all of which are wanting in solidity, but are otherwise interesting." In one of his letters to Spohr we find that his opinion has undergone considerable alteration. He says : " I have heard three Quartets " (op. 41) " by Schumann, the first that he has written, which pleased me very much; they caused me great astonishment concerning his talent, which I did not think so very remarkable when I heard some pianoforte things some time ago ; they were too condensed and scrappy, and constantly fell into mere eccentricity. Here, too, there is no lack of what is unusual, both in form and contents, but it is made and held together with great power, and much is very beautiful."

From Mendelssohn's strange silence on the subject of Schumann as a composer, it may safely be concluded that he did not appreciate him at his true value. He recognized Schumann's literary power and critical acumen, but failed altogether to realize his true greatness. Certain persons, who at one time devoted a great deal of attention to the search for any evidence that would prove the two greatest composers of their day to have cherished animosity against one another, made the most of the absence of Schumann's name from Mendelssohn's published letters, but happily there is plenty of proof that their relations were always

on the friendliest possible footing, though Mendelssohn
never repaid in kind the numberless tokens of Schumann's admiration, which were constantly appearing in
the *Neue Zeitschrift*.

For a number of years Sterndale Bennett, in like
manner, failed to appreciate Schumann's music; nor
is it hard to account for this, when we remember that
at the period when he enjoyed the closest personal
intimacy with the composer,[1] the years 1836 and 1837,
the latter had only written the earlier pianoforte
works, which were not at first received with any de-
monstrations of delight by the musical world. It was
not until the composer had been at rest for many
years that the eyes of his friend were opened to
the surpassing beauties of some of the finest works,
such as, for instance, the Symphonies and other orchestral compositions. Yet, although his admiration was
limited, he acted the part of a true and loyal friend to
Schumann, being among the first and most eager sup-
porters and promoters of his music in England. Many
of Schumann's most important works were heard for

[1] Some idea of this intimacy is given by the fact that, on
the occasion of one of those jovial evenings which were so frequently passed in the company of the composer, Bennett wrote
a little canon on the following words :—

"Herr Schumann ist ein guter Mann,
Er raucht Tabak als Niemand kann;
Ein Mann vielleicht von dreissig Jahr,
Mit kurze Nas' und kurze Haar."

("Herr Schumann is a first-rate man,
He smokes as ne'er another can;
A man of thirty, I suppose,
Short is his hair, and short his nose.")

the first time in London under Bennett's direction. Another most ardent pioneer of Schumann's was Mr. John Ella, who introduced nearly all the chamber music to an English audience at the concerts of the Musical Union. Mention must be made of the Philharmonic Society, at whose concerts at least two of the symphonic works, and "Paradise and the Peri" were brought out; also of the Cambridge University Musical Society, under whose auspices the pianoforte Concerto, the "Rheinweinlied" overture, and the "Scenes from Faust" (part III.) were first given in England. But the greatest meed of praise is due to the constant and indefatigable zeal of Mr. August Manns and Sir George Grove, who at the Crystal Palace concerts did much, the one by his intelligent and sympathetic interpretations, and the other by his able and appreciative analyses, to transform the attitude of the British public towards Schumann's orchestral works from one of scanty toleration to one of admiring sympathy.

The worst enemies to the progress of Schumann's popularity in this country were the leading musical critics, who set themselves systematically to pour contempt and even ridicule upon his works, whenever they were performed. Without quotations it would be impossible to give the reader any idea of the virulence or the intemperance of these attacks, but it is undesirable to give references by which the writers might be identified, more especially as those very organs in which the most abusive passages are to be found are those which have since been most closely identified with the cause of musical progress.

The attack began in a carefully indirect manner
in the course of a favourable notice of the " Album
fur die Jugend." "These pieces, which the recondite
and mystical composer of the ' Kreisleriana,' ' Paradise and the Peri,' and ' Genoveva,' would most
probably contemn as mere trifles,—shallow common-
places—foolish, *because* they are pleasing and intelligible,—are, on these very grounds, among the most
acceptable of Dr. Schumann's works. The writer's
grim and gloomy works on a large scale are liked only
by a small congregation of admirers, which, happily
for the health of musical society, does not increase."
This was in 1852. In the next year the same weekly
periodical published the following sapient criticism of
the Quintet : " We must give up Dr. Schumann if this
be his most agreeable work. Straightforward enough
it is, and less freaked (*sic*) by uglinesses than is usual
with him ; but in three of the four movements the
ideas are worn and stale, not to say frivolous. . . .
That which should be grand is only heavy,—that which
should be brilliant is only bustling,—that which should
flow, stagnates. . . . On the whole, unpleasing pre-
tention hiding real poverty occurs to us as the general
character of this quintet."

In the spring of the year in which her husband
died, Madame Schumann paid a visit to England, and
played, among other things, his Duet for two pianos
with Sterndale Bennett, and his pianoforte Concerto.
One of the critics, who was always good enough to
admire the lady's playing, approved to some extent of
the Duet, but spoke, in criticizing the Concerto, of the
" efforts of the gifted lady to make her husband's

curious rhapsody pass for music," and called "many of the bravura passages utterly extravagant." The reader who has felt the charm of the cross-rhythm in the finale of this work will be surprised to hear, from another critic, of " the rondo (*sic*) to his piano Concerto, where the monotonous limping of the second subject, in place of piquing the ear, harasses it by producing an effect of lameness which retards the animation of the movement."

In the way of sweeping assertions, the following are unsurpassed; they occur in a criticism on the Overture, Scherzo, and Finale (op. 52), when that work was produced at the Philharmonic concert of April 4th, 1853. "An affectation, a superficial knowledge of art, an absence of true expression, and an infelicitous disdain of form have characterized every work of Robert Schumann's hitherto introduced into this country. . . . The convulsive efforts of one who has never properly studied his art to hide the deficiencies of early education under a mist of pompous swagger. . . . The whole work is unworthy of analysis, since it has no merit whatever." In these years the orchestral compositions were uniformly treated with contempt. The Symphony in B flat is called by one critic " heaviness without pomp, and harshness without brilliancy." In a musical paper the Symphony in D minor is reviewed on two occasions, separated by the interval of a year, in terms which form, when read together, an amusing and instructive commentary on the worth of contemporary criticism. In 1857 we read, "A sort of trio to the quick movement in the romanza consists of gasping strains that may be likened to the final breathing of a dying fish. . . . The finale is more clear and rational, and for a very good reason,—the reminiscences of Beethoven are absurdly palpable." In the following year the same organ expresses its opinion that in the first movement "some discords . . . are enough to perpendicularize one's hair. In the finale these painful noises are again indulged in. We might put up with it to the end of the romanza, but beyond this point the patience of an audience should not be tried." The "infatuation" of Mr. Manns in producing the work is spoken of at the same time with much condolence.

From these critics nothing was sacred. After the terrible catastrophe of February 27th, 1854, when his attempt to commit suicide necessitated his being placed under restraint, it was deliberately asserted in a paper devoted to the interests of music, that he was suffering from an attack of delirium tremens !

On June 23rd, 1856, "Paradise and the Peri" was performed at a Philharmonic concert, by her Majesty's command, under the direction of Sterndale Bennett, and with Madame Lind-Goldschmidt in the principal part. This event was followed by an article in a prominent daily paper which, for vigour of vituperation and total disregard of truth, is happily without parallel in the annals of English musical criticism. It is impossible, without quoting the article *in extenso*, to convey an idea of the rancour of its spirit, but we must content ourselves with brief extracts. "Whatever has been presented from the studio of this illustrious composer has met with a fiasco. . . . He began nobly, as a critic and general writer upon music. But

most unhappily he began to compose himself,—a mission
for which nature had never pointed him out. . . . Quick
to detect the weakness of others, he failed to acknow-
ledge his own; and from small things to large (from
bad to worse), as blind impulse suggested and ambition drove him on, he became transformed by degrees
from one of the friends to one of the enemies of art.
For a long time Schumann stood at the head of a
phalanx of apostates, who were only arrested for a time
by the short but brilliant career of Mendelssohn from
exercising a pernicious influence throughout the length
and breadth of Germany. . . . A still more daring
and uncompromising innovator appearing, however,
in the person of Richard Wagner, Schumann from the
post of generalissimo subsided into one of the sub-
sidiary officers of the new 'school.' His vanity was
hurt; his egotism received a deadly blow. . . . Though
backward to admit this new prophet at the beginning,
he was compelled to do so at the end. The result is
patent to the world. Schumann went mad, and Wagner
reigned alone. . . . We have only to add that as a
musical composition it (i.e. 'Paradise and the Peri')
is destitute of invention and wanting in intelligible
form; that its melodic ideas are as vague and common-
place as its treatment, both for voices and instruments,
is unscholarlike. A less 'dainty dish' was assuredly
never 'set before the Queen.'" Referring to the
same concert in another place, the same critic remarks,
"Robert Schumann has had his innings, and been
bowled out,—like Richard Wagner. 'Paradise and
the Peri' has gone to the tomb of the 'Lohengrins.'"

The passage about the composer's ambition and

egotism is only equalled by the gratuitousness of the
assumption that his insanity was caused by jealousy
of Wagner. That the schools of these two composers
can ever have been considered as identical, seems to
us nowadays inconceivable ; they have diverged widely
enough in these later years to satisfy even the captious
critic whom we have just quoted, as is amply proved
by an utterance from the head-quarters of Wagnerism
concerning Schumann, which we shall presently have
to consider. The state of English opinion remained
very much the same, improving only by slow degrees,
until nearly ten years had elapsed since the composer's
death. The first sign of the general adoption of wiser
and broader views concerning Schumann was the
unanimously favourable reception of the " Rhenish "
Symphony when it was given at one of Signor Arditi's
concerts at Her Majesty's Theatre in 1865. From
that time onwards the fame of Schumann has steadily
increased, and his music has gradually made its way
to the hearts of all real lovers of music in our country.

The German attack on Schumann, to which we
have just alluded, is to be found in the number
of the *Bayreuther Blätter*—the organ of the extreme
Wagnerian party—for August, 1879. The importance
of the article is not so much due to anything which it
contains, as to the quarter from whence it comes. If
it could be conclusively proved to represent the
opinions of the master himself, a certain historical
interest would attach to it, but as there is nothing to
show that Wagner was to be held in any way responsible for what appeared in the periodical, it must
stand or fall on its own merits exclusively. Without

being known to fame himself, the writer bears a surname which has become celebrated throughout the musical world, and which therefore may be supposed to carry a certain degree of weight in musical matters. He poses as the defender of the classical composers against the onslaught of the "romanticist" Schumann, whose antagonism to their cause he is at infinite pains to establish. His line of argument would seem to be something like this: "The classicists and romanticists must be eternally antagonistic the one to the other; the former are all good, therefore the latter are all bad. But Schumann is a romanticist; he is therefore a bad composer." If we accept Coleridge's dictum that assertion is the strongest form of argument, we must admit the strength of this writer's position to be absolutely impregnable, for it relies wholly upon assertions, proof being apparently regarded as altogether superfluous. One of his assertions is as follows: " The great popularity of this author, if it lasts much longer, will render the understanding and enjoyment of all the classics of music difficult, if not indeed impossible." Until some explanation is kindly vouchsafed as to the manner in which the reputation of the great masters is to be injured, we must continue to think that their standing will not be materially imperilled by the duration, not to say increase of Schumann's fame. During the greater part of the article, the writer ignores altogether the possibility of any of Schumann's works being regarded as anything but "romantic." He implies, in one place, that some of the larger works may be considered to be in harmony with the "classical" rules, for he owns, in the most candid manner, to sympathizing with the celebrated sentiment of Caliph Omar, on the occasion of the burning of the Alexandrian Library, "that those books which were in agreement with the Koran were superfluous, and those in opposition to it pernicious." The writer is in happy ignorance that, if his own dictum were accepted and acted upon, all music written subsequently to the close of the "classical" age,—whenever that was,—would stand condemned, including the works of that master in whose honour the *Bayreuther Blätter* were founded.

As the Bayreuth attack was based, ostensibly, at least, upon an imagined antagonism between Schumann and classical composers, so the London attacks of twenty years before were really dictated by a desire to sweep away all suspected rivals from before the feet of the adored Mendelssohn. This may, in some measure, excuse the eagerness and bitterness of the critics, though their virulence and intemperance are unpardonable.

The fact that Mendelssohn's compositions were from their first appearance received with universal admiration, while those of Schumann have waited so long for general acceptation, is a direct consequence of the differing theories of art pursued by the two men. The former felt that nothing that could not at once appeal to the world in general was worth saying in music; the latter, that he must say that which was given him to say, whether the public understood him or not.

The temptation to compare the relative greatness of these two composers is strongest exactly at the time when it is most impossible that such a comparison could be justly instituted. We, even yet, stand too near them to be able to decide which is the greater of the two. Those who stand at the foot of a mountain cannot form a right judgment as to the comparative height of its peaks; with increasing distance the spectator's estimate becomes ever more and more just. So it is with our opinion of these masters. We are too much inclined to range ourselves on one side or another, according to our various artistic creeds; but music is justified of all her children, and we may rest assured, that high on the roll of her glorious sons, not far from the names of Bach and Beethoven, are writte those of Mendelssohn and Robert Schumann.

THE END.

K

CHRONOLOGICAL TABLE OF
ROBERT SCHUMANN'S LIFE AND WORKS.

| A.D. | AGE. | EVENTS OF HIS LIFE AND COMPOSITIONS. | PAGE |

"Papillons," op. 2, completed . . 15, 49, 50, 123
Allegro for pianoforte, op. 8.

1832. 22. Visit to Zwickau and Schneeberg in the winter.
Part of a symphony in G minor played at
Clara Wieck's concert at Zwickau (Nov. 18)   16

Six Intermezzi for pianoforte, op. 4 . . 16, 51
Studies after Paganini's caprices, Book I., op. 3. 16, 49
Nos. 1, 3, 12, 13, and 15 from "Albumblätter,"
op. 124.
Symphony in G minor, unpublished . . 16, 76

1833. 23. Return to Leipzig (Riedel's Garten, afterwards
Burgstrasse) 16, 17
Death of Rosalie Schumann (Oct.) . . . 17

Studies after Paganini's caprices, Book II.,
op. 10 . . . . 17, 49
Impromptus on an air of Clara Wieck, op. 5   17, 124
Toccata for pianoforte, op. 7 17
Sonata in G minor begun, op. 22 . . . 55

1834. 24. *Neue Zeitschrift* projected, and first number published (April 3). Death of Schunke (Dec. 7) 18, 22

Études Symphoniques, op. 13 . . 21, 22, 53, 54
Carnaval, op. 9, begun 21, 22

1835. 25. G minor symphony performed as a whole at
Zwickau 16
Mendelssohn comes to Leipzig (Oct.) . . 22

Carnaval, op. 9, finished . . . 22, 52, 53, 114
Sonata in F sharp minor, op. 11 . . 54, 55, 124
Sonata in G minor, op. 22, except last movement 55
Nos. 2, 4, 11, and 17 of "Albumblätter," op. 124.

1836. 26. Beginning of affection for Clara Wieck . . 23

Fantasia for pianoforte in C, op. 17 . . 55, 56
Sonata in F minor, op. 14. ("Concert pour piano-
forte seul") 56, 57, 124
Nos. 5 and 7 of "Albumblätter," op. 124, and
No. 6 of "Bunte Blätter," op. 99.

| A.D | AGE. | EVENTS OF HIS LIFE AND COMPOSITIONS. | PAGE |

Balladen und Romanzen for chorus, Book I., op.
67; Book II., op. 75; Book III., op. 145;
Book IV., op. 146.

Romances for female chorus, Book. I., op. 69 ;
Book II., op. 91.

Spanisches Liederspiel, op. 74 88

Five " Stücke im Volkston " for piano and violoncello, op. 102 73

Lieder-Album for the young, op. 79.

"Jagdlieder," five songs for male chorus and
four horns obbligato, op. 137 . . . 87

Motet " Verzweifle nicht," for double male
chorus, op. 93 87

"Minnespiel," from Rückert's "Liebesfrühling,"
op. 101. 88

Four marches for pianoforte, op. 76 . . . 60

No. 14 of op. 99.

Songs (nine) from " Wilhelm Meister," and " Requiem for Mignon " for chorus, op. 98 . 87

Cathedral, garden, and " Ariel " scenes from
" Faust " 94, 95

Four duets for soprano and tenor, op. 78.

Twelve pianoforte pieces (four hands), op. 85.

Introduction and Allegro for pianoforte and
orchestra, op. 92 74

Four songs for double chorus, op. 141.

" Nachtlied " (Hebbel), for chorus and orchestra
op. 108 . . . . 87, 88

Spanische Liebeslieder, op. 138 . . . 88

Three songs (Byron's Hebrew Melodies) for one
voice, with harp or piano accompaniment,
op. 95.

Three Romances for oboe and piano, op. 94 . 73

"Schön Hedwig," ballad for declamation (Hebbel), op. 106.

1850. 40. Concert tour to Leipzig, Bremen, and Hamburg
(spring) 37

Production of " Genoveva," (June 25) . . 38

Appointment to Düsseldorf, in Hiller's place,
and removal there (September) . . 37, 38

" Neujahrslied" (Rückert) for chorus and orchestra, op. 144 98

Three songs, op. 83.

Works of Uncertain Date.

INDEX.